UNVEILED BY GOD

DISCOVER THE BEAUTY
OF WHO YOU REALLY ARE

UNVEILED
BY GOD
TERESA YANCY

m.

ISBN Paperback: 978-1-953314-18-5

ISBN Ebook: 978-1-953314-20-8

Library of Congress Control Number: 2021913731

Published by:

Messenger Books
30 N. Gould Ste. R
Sheridan, WY 82801

messenger
BOOKS

CONTENTS

"You saw who you created me to be before I became me!"
—Psalm 139:16a, TPT—

———

*"We can all draw close to him with the veil removed from our faces.
And with no veil we all become like mirrors who brightly reflect the glory
of the Lord Jesus. We are being transfigured into his very image as we
move from one brighter level of glory to another. And this glorious
transfiguration comes from the Lord, who is the Spirit."*
—2 Corinthians 3:18, TPT—

I dedicate this book to my four greatest treasures: my children. Josiah, Moriah, Grace, and Promise, you are my powerful motivation for dismantling the strongholds of the enemy in my life.

You are worth the price.

I bless you with freedom, peace, and the pleasure of loving God with an undivided heart—with all your heart, all your mind, and all your strength.

Now run your races and satisfy your King with lives well lived in passionate pursuit of the one thing that matters: friendship with Him. I will be right here on the sidelines cheering you on!

You are my why.

INTRODUCTION

"The Word of the Lord came to me saying: 'Before I formed you in the womb I knew you; before you were born I sanctified you.'"

—Jeremiah 1:4-5, NKJV

"You formed my innermost being, shaping my delicate inside and my intricate outside, and wove them all together in my mother's womb. I thank you, God, for making me so mysteriously complex! Everything you do is marvelously breathtaking. It simply amazes me to think about it! How thoroughly you know me, Lord! You even formed every bone in my body when you created me in the secret place, carefully, skillfully shaping me from nothing to something. You saw who you created me to be before I became me! Before I'd ever seen the light of day, the number of days you planned for me were already recorded in your book."

— Psalms 139:13-16, TPT

You and I are each a thought of God. Before you were conceived in your mother's womb, you were in the heart of God. He imagined you, then He formed you. No matter what circumstances you were born into or what parents contributed your DNA, you were first a dream in the heart of the Creator. You are no accident. You are no byproduct. You are an intentional creation of God Himself. Father thought you, planned you, recorded His plans for you in His book, and then formed you. You are His design, His masterpiece, and subsequently, you are truly priceless.

Every parent knows the awe and wonder of holding their newborn baby for the first time. There is no earthly experience quite like it. Holding any newborn is joyous, but it can't compare to holding our very own. We will shamelessly hold and coddle our newborns just simply gazing upon them. They cannot communicate with us or give us anything, but we are more than satisfied just to simply feast our eyes on them, marveling over each finger, each dimple, and each coo. We literally adore them.

In my own family, we have four children and have often joked that those precious moments are quite nearly idolatry. We just can't get enough! If that is how we humans react to the experience of becoming a parent, how much more so does Father God! We are not just one of many; we are each special, unique, and achingly adored by God.

Sadly, most people (even Christians) do not experience His adoration. Circumstances, relationships, difficulties, and painful life experiences have taught us a different picture of God and of ourselves. Unfortunately we learn to relate to our Heavenly Father as if He is so much less passionate about us. We may believe He loves us, but many can hardly imagine Him liking us, really and truly *liking* us. We exchange the truth about God and His character of unconditional, deep and wide love, for a lie of a temperamental God who is unaffected, unavailable, and inattentive.

Of course, as faithful, church going, Bible believing Christians, we would never consciously admit to ourselves that we are ensnared in such lies. We could probably quote chapter and verse from the Bible and vehemently disprove every one of them, but that wouldn't and doesn't change the fact that our image of God may indeed be marred and in need of repair.

I truly believe we are in a time when God is restoring us through true revelation of His unconditional love. My prayer for you as you read this book is that you will fully come to know Him as the unconditional lover of your soul. I pray that you will rediscover the secret place where He first encountered you and stamped you with His image, and that you will learn to abide there continually, not out of duty or fear, but out of passion and love.

I pray you will see what He saw when He imagined you, and that you will live out of that identity. Is it a requirement that you understand these things in order to enter heaven? No, but they are His ultimate intention for you. You interfaced with God when He formed you. You will never be truly fulfilled or fulfill His plans until you allow Him to take you through the wondrous process of unveiling the beauty of who you really are. He alone has the keys that will unlock you and cause you to become.

> "'For I know the plans I have for you,' declares the Lord, 'plans to prosper you and not to harm you, plans to give you hope and a future. Then you will call on me and come and pray to me, and I will listen to you. You will seek me and find me when you seek me with all your heart. I will be found by you,' declares the Lord, 'and will bring you back from captivity.'"
>
> —Jeremiah 29:11-14a, NIV

"So I kneel humbly in awe before the Father of our Lord Jesus, the Messiah, the perfect Father of every father and child in heaven and on the earth. And I pray that he would unveil within you the unlimited riches of his glory and favor until supernatural strength floods your innermost being with his divine might and explosive power. Then, by constantly using your faith, the life of Christ will be released deep inside you, and the resting place of his love will become the very source and root of your life. Then you will be empowered to discover what every holy one experiences—the great magnitude of the astonishing love of Christ in all its dimensions. How deeply intimate and far-reaching is his love! How enduring and inclusive it is! Endless love beyond measurement that transcends our understanding—this extravagant love pours into you until you are filled to overflowing with the fullness of God!

Never doubt God's mighty power to work in you and accomplish all this. He will achieve infinitely more than your greatest request, your most unbelievable dream, and exceed your wildest imagination! He will outdo them all, for his miraculous power constantly energizes you. Now we offer up to God all the glorious praise that rises from every church in every generation through Jesus Christ—and all that will yet be manifest through time and eternity. Amen."

— EPHESIANS 3:14-21, TPT

Prayer

Father God, I believe that You accurately see me, that You fully know me, and that You deeply love me. I believe that You are truly for me, and that You are my greatest supporter.

As I read this book, help me to be able to see myself the way that You do. Help me to also see You clearly. Give me a healthy and pure vision of who You truly are. Above all, help me to know You more. Let me see Your glory. Lord, I really need a friend like You. Help me to develop a closer friendship with You and a deeper connection with You. Give me grace to be a better friend to You as well. No one could ever be more worthy, so show me how to do my part to make that possible.

I choose to give myself to this pursuit. Open the eyes of my heart, dear God. I draw near to You, and, even if at times it feels like baby steps, I know You delight in those steps. Your Word promises that You are, right now, at this very moment, also drawing near to me. Thank You so much for that.

Lord, I want to tell You now that my response to You is yes. *Whatever You ask, my answer is yes, because I am done with fear, shame, and all low level living. I want wholeness. I want it all, Lord. I want the total package and the fullness of all that Your blood purchased for me: righteousness, peace, and joy.*

Therefore, I choose to yield to You and allow You to do what only You can do. Heal me, free me, fill me, and cause me to become the dream You have dreamt for my life. I ask You for all this in the Name of Jesus, and I thank You in advance. Amen.

PART 1

UNVEILING BEAUTY — Who You Really Are

Christlikeness is the hope of glory within us, and we yearn deeply for that reality. From the moment we receive Christ, we are on a journey of becoming like Him and one with Him. And there is a veil of shame that must be discarded along the way.

In this section, we will discuss the truth that Glory—Christlikeness —is your destiny, and the unveiling of your true identity is at hand. Don't yield to discouragement because of the residual shame of your past. Your past sins are erased, and your new life is one of complete rest in God's great love as you grow and go from glory to glory to glory.

1

THE IMAGO: THE TRUE YOU

"We can all draw close to him with the veil removed from our faces. And with no veil we all become like mirrors who brightly reflect the glory of the Lord Jesus. We are being transfigured into his very image as we move from one brighter level of glory to another. And this glorious transfiguration comes from the Lord, who is the Spirit."

— 2 CORINTHIANS 3:18, TPT

When a caterpillar turns into a butterfly, the transformation is so radical that it's hard to believe they belong to the same species. However, regardless of the new wings and body, the new diet, and the new airborne lifestyle, scientists have found that butterflies remember what they learned as caterpillars! This tells me that the caterpillar is not gone but rather it is radically changed.

It Is a *Transformation* not an Extermination.

The essence of the caterpillar and the butterfly is the same. It is simply transformed, freed from lowly living, and lifted to its true identity.

The adult stage of a butterfly is called the imago and is also referred to as the imaginal stage. The imago is the *image* of the original design that was just waiting to be released, *but it was always there.* Always. Similarly, *imago dei* is a theological term for God's people that comes from Genesis 1:27 where we are told that God made man in His image. This is how our creator God *sees* us--the true us, the imago. As His beloved children, we thrill His heart, and if we let Him, He will unveil us for His glory.

> "...in this twilight darkness I know I am so unworthy—so in need. Yet you are so lovely! I feel as dark and dry as the desert tents of the wandering nomads. Yet you are so lovely— like the fine linen tapestry hanging in the Holy Place...Won't you tell me, lover of my soul, where do you feed your flock? Where do you lead your beloved ones to rest in the heat of the day? For I wish to be wrapped all around you as I wander among the flocks of your shepherds. It is you I long for, with no veil between us"
>
> — SONG OF SONGS 1:5-7, TPT

This revealing passage from the greatest song of all perfectly illustrates the dynamic of our relationship with Christ. We may accurately see our imperfections, our dark and dry places, but He sees us for who we truly are and says adoringly over us, "Yet you are so lovely!"

He has *chosen* us, and His choice overrides all else. Mercy, His great love, triumphs over judgment.

We are all familiar with the churchy rhetoric of false humility that basically leads us to feel that we are nothing and that we should despise our humanity. The truth is that God made us human, and

He clothes our humanity with His glory, His very self. This is beautifully illustrated by the furniture in the tabernacle in the wilderness.
All the pieces of furniture were wood, earthly, but were overlaid
with pure gold. Why didn't the God who is limitless in power and
riches simply have them made fully of gold? One reason, I believe,
is that it is an inspiring message to every lover of God that we are
His precious, useful, beloved masterpieces. Our humanity is united
with His divine nature (pure gold) in Christ. Just as the ark of the
covenant was covered within and without (completely) so are we. We
are perfectly covered by love and therefore have absolutely nothing
to fear.

God is not trying to get rid of you. He's not moving you out of the
way. It's not less of you and more of Him. He's not even decreasing
you and increasing Himself (although we understand the intention
of this teaching). He's not emptying you of you, so He can fill you
with Himself, or any of the euphemisms that go on and on.

He actually likes you! Just as any good father would, and of course, He
is the best! He wants to bring you up out of any muck and mire,
clean you, and polish you so that the truth of who you really are in
Him shines through. He wants to see you grow and flourish and
mature to a place of partnership *with* Him. Oh yes, that is His heart.
He wants to see His children arise and shine with His glory upon
them and *through* them (not in spite of them); He will cover the
whole earth with His glory!

> "Arise, shine; for your light has come, And the glory of the LORD
> has risen upon you. "For behold, darkness will cover the earth And
> deep darkness the peoples; But the LORD will rise upon you And
> His glory will appear upon you."
>
> — ISAIAH 60:1-2, NASB

Be still for a moment. Recognize His sweet, loving presence all
around you and rest there. Can't you just sense how He delights in
you? He is *for* you, not against you. He will never leave you nor

forsake you. That's His great promise, and it holds. He has bound His heart to you. It is His covenant with you, and He doesn't ever break covenant. His love is upon you, and His love reaches past all of eternity. He will never change His mind about you. He is constant.

Loving-Kindness

"The Lord appeared from of old to me [Israel], saying, Yes, I have loved you with an everlasting love; therefore with loving-kindness have I drawn you and continued My faithfulness to you."

— Jeremiah 31:3, AMPC

Loving-kindness is actually a word that is peculiar to the Bible. It is a word that translators invented to convey the rich and layered meaning of the Hebrew word, *hesed*. Hesed means love but also so much more! It is a covenant love similar to marriage. It connotes faithfulness. It is a love that holds on and on and on.

God is a just God. This aspect of His nature demands justice and righteousness. However, hesed, His covenant love, overrides justice and triumphs. His faithful, covenant love (His loving-kindness) will never fail you, no matter what. In fact, you could never fail so greatly that you cause His great love to fail. You are not that powerful.

"But even if we are faithless, He will still be full of faith, for he never wavers in his faithfulness to us."

— 2 Timothy 2:13, TPT

Imagine if a lost work of a master artist like Da Vinci were to be discovered. Even if it were marred by the dirt or damage of time, it would *never* be discarded, quite the opposite! Someone would patiently, painstakingly, and passionately labor to *restore* its beauty. Its value though, would never be in question.

It would be insane to even momentarily consider tearing out that old canvas and replacing it to repaint a different design.

Unfortunately, this is how many of us feel about ourselves.

However, it is *not* how God feels.

He is the great artist of our lives. He is committed to restoring the original design, but He loves us just as we are because we are His workmanship. And, because *He* is our designer, you and I have *great* worth; we're priceless actually. Only the blood of God could purchase us.

> "Have you forgotten that your body is now the sacred temple of the Spirit of Holiness, who lives in you? You don't belong to yourself any longer, for the gift of God, the Holy Spirit, lives inside your sanctuary. You were God's expensive purchase, paid for with tears of blood, so by all means, then, use your body to bring glory to God."
>
> — 1 CORINTHIANS 6:19-20, TPT

Now, why would He pay such a price only to get rid of you, hide you, dismiss you, diminish you, or decrease you? Of course we must die to our sinful desires, that's a given; however, your personality and your soul He treasures.

Love's Response

Have you ever heard of the cold shoulder or the silent treatment? This is a common tactic used in relationships to get our own way or manipulate others to do or not do what we desire. Sadly, it is quite effective. One reason for its great effectiveness and proliferate use is that it actually inflicts real pain. Studies show that this type of rejection, isolation, and withholding of affection causes the same response in the brain as physical abuse. To put it plainly, it hurts badly. In fact, so much so, that many of us would rather feel a physical pain than the pain of abandonment and rejection.

Why do I bring this up? Because it is important for us to realize that the cold shoulder of rejection is not the way our Heavenly Father disciplines or deals with us. He is the very One who has promised to never leave or forsake us. Amazingly, He molds our character and teaches us His beautiful ways *through intimacy*, not isolation.

Also, in the same way that I love each of the unique characteristics of my four children, God gets a kick out of His kids. He *enjoys* them. Here is something truly mind-blowing: I love *all* the aspects of my children, even their weaknesses. In fact, it is *within* the unique fallibilities of their individual personalities that my compassion and love for them finds its *greatest* expression. It makes me want to love them *more*. How amazing that their frailties evoke my love, not revoke it.

How much wider and deeper is Father God's unfathomable love for us? So again, I believe there is a much greater plan at work here. God is not out to make an army of clones, robots, or even fear led drudges. He is making for Himself a *crown of glory*, a *holy family!* We are His sons and daughters who walk this world in purity (not perfection), spreading everywhere the fragrance and light of Christ. It's a *high* calling. He must think highly of us. Let's think His thoughts.

"God always makes his grace visible in Christ, who includes us as partners of his endless triumph. Through our yielded lives he spreads the fragrance of the knowledge of God everywhere we go.

We have become the unmistakable aroma of the victory of the Anointed One to God—a perfume of life to those being saved and the odor of death to those who are perishing."

— 2 CORINTHIANS 2:14-15, TPT

"I admit that I haven't yet acquired the absolute fullness that I'm pursuing, but I run with passion into his abundance so that I may reach the purpose that Jesus Christ has called me to fulfill and wants me to discover. I don't depend on my own strength to accomplish this; however I do have one compelling focus: I forget all of the past as I fasten my heart to the future instead. I run straight for the divine invitation of reaching the heavenly goal and gaining the victory-prize through the anointing of Jesus."

— PHILIPPIANS 3:12-14, TPT

Summary

- When God looks at you, He sees your imago. He sees you as you truly are, and He likes you!
- Father is committed to your *full restoration*. You are His masterpiece, and He will never abandon the good work that He has begun in you.
- God thinks beautiful, high, and perfect thoughts about you. Your frailties, weaknesses, and scars evoke the greatest expressions of His love.
- Scriptures for deeper study: Isaiah 60:1-2; 1 Corinthians 6:19-20; 2 Corinthians 2:14-15; Philippians 3:12-14

Prayer

Father, in the past I have thought and believed things about myself that are not in line with Your love for me. I am sorry for that, and I repent. I also repent for any way that I have hated myself or rejected myself. Please forgive me, Lord. Right now I choose to align my will with Your will. I choose to accept myself and to embrace my "imago", Your image of me. I trust You to reveal that true and healthy image to me more and more. I ask You to make it clearer and clearer every day of my life, and that through my life You would spread Your fragrance, love, and glory to the world. Amen.

Faith Declaration

"God could not love me any *more* or *better* than He does right now. I am *completely* loved."

Activation

Set aside some quiet time with God, and ask these questions. Wait for His answers, and write them down.

- What lie am I believing about myself? What is the truth?
- What lie am I believing about my past (experiences, mistakes, or failures)? What is the truth?
- What lie am I believing about my future? What is the truth?
- Father, what do You think of me?

HE RESTORES MY SOUL

"As he [a person] thinks in his heart, so is he…"

— PROVERBS 27:3A, NKJV

The Mind–Heart Connection

This scripture reveals an important connection: the *connection between the mind and heart*. We are triune: body, soul, spirit. Our soul consists of the mind (thoughts), will (choices), and emotions (feelings). The will is where choices are made, and these choices make, or *create*, our life. Our lives *become* the choices we make, because the choices we make truly make up our lives. Whether referring to the little choices we make throughout the day or the big life choices that bring major shifts, either way, big or small, *all* of our choices direct and define our lives. It is so important, therefore, to examine those things which precipitate or lead us to the choices we make.

The Real Question

The question is this: Why do we do the things we do? Obviously, if we automatically made the right choices consistently, our life would be awesome. I mean really, if we could hear God's truth on a matter and then immediately make all of our thoughts and actions perfectly line up with the truth that we have heard and believed, we would always be victorious!

Well, it doesn't quite happen that way does it? No, instead we are in a *process of transformation*, and, as much as we may wish for a quicker fix, *usually* change occurs gradually as God's word and truth is worked into the fabric of our souls. Our life transformation progresses as we grow from truth that we know in our head, to truth that we know in our heart.

Important Keys:

- The battle is in our mind for our will.

- Our emotions are actually wellness indicators.

- When I am winning in my thoughts, I make good choices.

- When I make good choices, I have great peace (the fruit of the Spirit flowing, the peaceful fruit of righteousness per Hebrews 12).

So, as we consider the soul again, we see the will as our decision making place, and the *influencers* of the will are the mind and the emotions. Another model that we can overlay this concept with is this: the conscious mind is influenced by the subconscious mind.

Scientifically, we know that our mind is (at least) 80% subconscious.[1] Wow. Just think about that for a moment. 80% of our thought life (our soul) is operating on a *subconscious* level. *This is why we need inner healing.* Go ahead and read that again. Yes, inner healing provides a *necessary detox* of inferior and unhealthy activity within our soul.

This 80% of our soul is a storage bank of memories and information that we hold, or file, on a subconscious level. We live our lives under the subconscious influence of this storage bank. God's Word teaches us that we are transformed by the renewing of our minds. Is this only the *conscious* mind? Of course it's not. Transformation takes place by the renewing of 100% of our minds--conscious and subconscious.

It isn't the truth that we understand *conceptually* that we live by. *It is the truth we believe in our hearts that we live from.* Again, scripture tells us, "As [a man] thinks, so is he." Obviously transformation must take place on a deeper level than mere mental agreement with truth; it must become *heart-level* truth. It must feel true. It must be revelation knowledge that we actually live from.

Don't misunderstand. Truth is truth whether or not it *feels* true. My point here is that if truth *doesn't* feel true to you, then there is a lie at work in the soul (buried in that 80%) that is *blocking* transformational, revelation knowledge that empowers you to overcome.

> "'But you—who do you say that I am?' Jesus asked. Simon Peter spoke up and said, 'You are the Anointed One, the Son of the living God!' Jesus replied, 'You are favored and privileged Simeon, son of Jonah! For you didn't discover this on your own, but my Father in heaven has supernaturally revealed it to you. I give you the name Peter, a stone. And this truth of who I am will be the bedrock foundation on which I will build my church—my legislative assembly, and the power of death will not be able to overpower it! I will give you the keys of heaven's kingdom realm to forbid on earth that which is forbidden in heaven, and to release on earth that which is released in heaven.'"

> — MATTHEW 16:15-19, TPT

This verse sums up our calling. In order to walk in revelation knowledge, intimacy, and authority in greater and greater fullness and fruitfulness, we must have greater and greater truth in our inward parts.

> "The spirit God breathed into man is like a living lamp, a shining light searching into the innermost chamber of our being."
>
> — PROVERBS 20:27, TPT

> "I know that you delight to set your truth deep in my spirit. So come into the hidden places of my heart and teach me wisdom."
>
> — PSALMS 51:6,TPT

I love that! I am His. You are His. He will not leave us unfinished. He will "teach me wisdom," because I am His workmanship. He is both the author and finisher...of us. He also sees our hearts. He loves our hearts. He is perfecting our hearts, from the inside out. He wants truth laid there, in our inward parts, so that we as His dearly loved children are able to live from a very firm foundation.

Now, surely we all know how important foundations are to the integrity of a structure. There is no lasting stability without that solid foundation. It is the exact same with each of us. We are meant for this stability and integrity. When the mind to heart connection is in sync, there is integrity. Integrity means *same*. When what I know in my head matches, or is the same, as what I know in my heart, something beautiful results: rock-solid peace. The ultimate "three-fold cord" then occurs when we can add obedience. Jesus taught that when we obey (in our will) the truth that we know (in our mind and heart) we are practically invincible.

> "Everyone who hears my teaching and applies it to his life can be compared to a wise man who built his house on an unshakable foundation. When the rains fell and the flood came, with fierce

winds beating upon his house, it stood firm because of its strong foundation."

— MATTHEW 7:24-25, TPT

Therefore, soul restoration occurs when truth comes into our innermost being. The right information must come in (Bible study, prayer, worship, meditation, etc.) and any wrong information (lies that block truth) must be exposed, removed, and replaced.

Renewing the Mind

When I first started walking with the Lord, I was voraciously hungry for God's word. Hunger is a sign of thriving. Lack of hunger is a symptom that we are not thriving. This is especially true for a baby, including a baby Christian.

I craved God's word and even carried my Bible with me to places like my college classes, restaurants, and work (this was before smartphones). Yes, I made my friends and family a bit concerned! They were worried that I had gone too far with this "Jesus stuff," but I knew that I needed to be feeding my spirit with a constant flow of life and truth. I was not trying to impress anybody by flashing my Bible everywhere. Rather, I simply knew how empty, sad, and powerless my previous walk had been even as a church-attending, God-fearing believer. In short, I had already been my own way (been there done that), and I knew it was not enough. I wanted the fullness of intimacy with Jesus. I still do. I believe it is what He paid for at Calvary. I still do.

Before long, I was amazed to find that God's Word would bubble up in my spirit at strategic and timely moments. I would be tempted to respond wrongly or with a bad attitude, and a scripture would come to my mind to counsel me. Or I would be talking to someone about the Lord, and just the perfect verse would come into my heart to share with them. I was so excited! I was seeing the results of my

Bible studying. I was experiencing very simply what God's word promises will happen.

> "Stop imitating the ideals and opinions of the culture around you, but be inwardly transformed by the Holy Spirit through a total reformation of how you think. This will empower you to discern God's will as you live a beautiful life, satisfying and perfect in his eyes."
>
> — ROMANS 12:2, TPT

A Key to Victory

Our lives must be built on God's Truth. That is foundational and irrefutable, but I want to take this a bit further for our discussion here concerning transformation.

Jesus said, "You will know the truth and the truth will set you free" (John 8:32, NIV). Well, okay. I know a lot of truth. Probably you do, too. In fact, I have read the Bible many times, however (and this is a BIG however), I am not yet walking in the freedom of all the truth I *know*. Why is that?

This is possibly the most important question for us to ponder. It is *the* issue for all of our issues.

How do I get the truth that I know in my head to be the truth that I know in my heart?

It is not enough that we can mentally agree to what God says in His word. We must know it to be true in our hearts. Ultimately, it is the truth that we know in our heart that truly makes us free like Jesus said.

So, how do we get it from our head to our heart? We realize there are many ways that God does this. He is so magnificent, wise, and powerful. He is not limited to a formula, a method, or a ritual. He actually counsels us this way:

> "Call upon me and I will answer you and show you great and mighty things which you know not. You shall seek me and you shall find me when you search for me with all your heart. I will be found by you says the Lord."

> — JEREMIAH 33:3, KJV

If we are hungry for truth, we will seek Him and find Him. He is not withholding anything from us. The Bible tells us that He is not keeping good things from us: "No good thing will he withhold from them that walk uprightly" (Ps. 84:11, NKJV).

It is God's good pleasure to give us the kingdom.[2] So, what is the kingdom? The kingdom of God is righteousness, peace, and joy in the Holy Spirit.[3]

> "Blessed are those who hunger and thirst for righteousness for they shall be filled."

> — MATTHEW 5:6, NKJV

If we are on that path of seeking Christ, *then we will find Him* and continually be transformed from glory to glory, guaranteed. He accomplishes it over time by His presence, His word, the prayers of others, the gifts and manifestations of the Spirit, asking, seeking, knocking, divine encounters, and so on.

Our assignment from heaven is to abide in Him and stay in the process. Many times when I have found myself in the crucible of change, my heart will desperately cry out for God to show me the way, because in those intense moments I feel a little lost. Then I hear His gentle whisper, "Teresa, I am the way. Draw near, because all the answers are in Me." He is saying that to you today as well.

Lies That Block Truth

I want to focus on one way in particular that God does His work of transformation in our souls: inner healing and deliverance. *We need inner healing and freedom from the wounds and lies that block us from knowing God's truth in a transformational way.*

Let me give you an example that shows how healing in our soul brings transformation to our life. My father abandoned our family (my mother and six children) when I was eleven years old. I never saw him again. Obviously, the ramifications of such a traumatic event are huge. Children are not really equipped to process something like this. Instead, we internalize it or stuff down our feelings. It may become filed in our young minds as basic (so-called) truths such as:

- "I am unlovable."
- "People who love me will eventually leave me."
- "There is something deeply wrong with me."
- "I'm not normal."
- "I can't count on people or men."

For me, I internalized many of those lies. One in particular really affected my relationship with God. I was profoundly afraid that God would abandon me. You may think that is silly to even consider. We all *know* that God is good. He is a good Father. Scripture even declares that He will never leave or forsake us (Heb. 13:5).

Let me tell you, I truly, *with all my heart* wanted to feel that security of *knowing* that God would always be there for me. But still, the deeply rooted fear abandonment would grip my heart at times. It was irrational. I knew better in my head, but my heart was silently screaming a different reality. I couldn't seem to reconcile the two "truths." *I needed to be healed.*

As I grew in my relationship with the Lord, I began to experience more and more freedom from this particular fear. I experienced His faithfulness over and over, and as I meditated on God's Word, the lie had less and less power; the stronghold was being torn down. Along the way, however, I also picked up some unhealthy tools. One resulting coping mechanism that I had to deal with was perfectionism. Because I feared abandonment so intensely, I worked really hard at being perfect. Obviously that is a losing battle!

The desire to be perfect wasn't a conscious decision. This is so important to understand. It was subconscious. It came from the inside, *where the lies are.* Even though I was getting accurate outside information from God's word and sound teaching, my perceived inner truth (which was a house of lies, the stronghold from which the spirit of fear positioned itself and attacked me continually) was that God might abandon me. So, when I blew it, I became fearful. If I wasn't doing enough for God, I became fearful. If a spiritual leader didn't like me, I became fearful. When I went through tough trials or storms, I was fearful. And on and on it went; it was a cycle of torment.

Maybe you identify with my experience. Unfortunately, we live in a world where people fail us. Abandonment and covenant breaking is epidemic. Nowadays it is practically the norm to say, "I never knew my father."

We are almost to the point where we are made to feel as if we should be able to shrug it off and just get over it. This is actually the total opposite of what we need to do. We need help and healing, not denial. This is a problem that obviously exists both within and without the body of Christ, and as the lighthouse in this dark world, the church should be shining brightly with hope and real solutions. Sadly, this is often not the case.

I grew up in a church where it seemed real issues like this were not actually dealt with. I basically felt like I would have to just be broken until I got to heaven. Issues (sins, problems, inner wounds, etc.) were things we just didn't talk about. It seemed they were just meant to be swept under the great spiritual rug of religion and ignored as if that is even remotely possible! The result of this mindset produces religious Christians. Hide your faults, keep things hush-hush, don't ask for help, just grit your teeth and wait for the sweet by and by.

I don't think I need to point out how far below the spiritual poverty line this type of living is. This is so *not* what Jesus died on the cross to obtain for us.

> "The reason the Son of God was revealed was to undo and destroy the works of the devil."
>
> — 1 JOHN 3:8, TPT

Jesus didn't endure death, hell, and the grave for us to be bound in fear. He redeemed you and I, and that doesn't simply mean a ticket to heaven after we die. It means redemption *now*, on earth, as it is in heaven. All our sins and the consequences of them have been redeemed. He certainly didn't pay the price that He paid so that we would partner with defeat. Therefore, the first step to freedom is recognizing that we aren't free, and that Jesus wants us free, to the uttermost.

> "So he is able to save fully [to the uttermost] from now throughout eternity, everyone who comes to God through him, because he lives to pray continually for them."
>
> — HEBREWS 7:25, TPT

Realizing that Jesus wants me to be free and also that freedom is possible was key to my transformation. Having grown up in the church, I had sung hymns my entire life that referred to our victory in Jesus, but had truly believed that real victory was only possible on "some glad morning when this life is o'er." Jesus's message was and is, however, very different! He came that we might have and enjoy life, and have it in abundance, to the full, until it overflows.[4] Abundance is our portion!

I didn't experience a one-time event of miraculous deliverance, although I believe in those. God took me through a process, as He often does. I don't know all the reasons why that is, but *I am thankful for the process.* I wouldn't be writing this right now if it hadn't been for the process.

I learned a lot through the process, and now I can share it with others to hopefully help them on their journey to freedom. I also found out something about the mysteries of transformation. Just like the butterfly in its chrysalis needs a safe place to hang while it is in the process, God is my safe place! He is your safe place as well.

He loves us just the way we are while we are in the process.

We are hidden, covered, and safe in the process.

> "Pillars of smoke, like silver mist— a canopy of golden glory dwells above it. The place where they sit together is sprinkled with crimson. Love and mercy cover this carriage, blanketing his tabernacle throne. The king himself has made it for those who will become his bride."
>
> — Song of Songs 3:10, TPT

Our Bridegroom King has us hidden in glory and sprinkled with crimson. We are His redemption prize. His love and mercy blanket us, His bride, as we are in the process of becoming ready for the wedding.

We don't have to be perfect, because we are *perfectly* loved. We are surrounded by the chrysalis of His presence, hidden in the cleft of the rock, sheltered in the secret place, under the shadow of His wings. In that place, we can be still and listen to His heartbeat of passionate love for us. We can *know* (not in our mind alone, but deep in our heart) that we are *profoundly treasured.*

A Picture of the Process

I am a certified elementary teacher. Once, for a science class, we had a caterpillar to butterfly activity. We bought the caterpillars and watched them grow (quadruple really), attach themselves to the roof of the jar, and form their chrysalises. We then transferred them very delicately to a large net and waited for them to emerge. This takes several days.

One Saturday, when it was nearing time for them to break free, I just happened to go to my classroom. It was not common for me to be in my classroom on the weekend (it was a fluke), but I peeked in on them and saw one chrysalis had fallen.

At first, I thought, "Oh well, just one loss. Not too bad." Then I went back and read the instructions, and it said that if one falls, gently place a napkin underneath it, because it may still be able to survive. So, that's what I did, but I really held little hope for this particular pupa.

The following Monday I came in to work and checked on the fallen one. It had indeed emerged from its chrysalis but was stuck in the goo that also comes out of the chrysalis when it opens. The poor butterfly was helplessly flopping on the bottom of the net unable to get its new wings free.

I wasn't sure what to do. I knew I probably shouldn't touch it, so I gently tapped on the underside of the net. After a few taps, the butterfly was able to break free of the wet slime and began to fly. I felt like I had witnessed a mini-miracle! It really wasn't supposed to be flying. The odds had totally been against this bug, but here it was, flying around like it didn't even know it wasn't supposed to.

Wow, isn't this like most of us? I know I feel like that butterfly. I know I shouldn't be fit to fly. My wings were certainly encumbered with plenty of muck and mire from life's hard knocks, but Jesus saw me. He had already seen the imago even before He formed me in the womb. He believed in me. He helped me when I couldn't help myself. If we could set *ourselves* free, we wouldn't need Jesus. But He is able to save (Greek: *sozo*) us to the uttermost, as the Bible says. *Sozo* means to save, heal, and deliver. He doesn't do anything halfway.

There are so many beautiful analogies for us to draw from this story.

God is our safe place to hang while we are in the process of transformation.

Also, while we are in the process, if we fall, He won't throw us out. No way. *He will give us **even more** special attention because we **need** it.*

Wherever there is less than abundance, Jesus wants to help and heal us. Wherever there is hopelessness, there is a lie in operation. Once we were completely without hope. Before Jesus lifted us up, we were sinking and going down for the count, but no longer! It is time to get your hopes up. You are coming up, out, and into your inheritance!

> "Living within you is the Christ who floods you with the expectation of glory! This mystery of Christ, embedded within us, becomes a heavenly treasure chest of hope filled with the riches of glory for his people, and God wants everyone to know it."
>
> — Colossians 1:27, TPT

> "For we continue to look forward to the joyful fulfillment of our hope in the dawning splendor of the glory of our great God and Savior, Jesus, the Anointed One."
>
> — Titus 2:13, TPT

Just like any loving parent, Father God is profoundly moved by our need. We don't ever have to be ashamed of our needs. We must simply bring our needs to Him. The alternative is trying to get our needs met in unhealthy ways, and isn't that exactly where all the negative, detrimental, and harmful cycles begin in our lives? We will talk more about that next.

Summary

- It is not just the truth that I know in my head but the truth that is also written on my heart that makes me free.
- In order for truth to replace lies in my heart, I may need inner healing from painful past experiences and traumas.
- At least 80% of my thought life is on a subconscious level which is a powerful filing system of all my life experiences.
- This 80% influences my mind, will, and emotions at all times.
- God can expose lies and reveal truth and set me free. One of the main ways He does this is through His word.
- God loves me just as I am *while* I am in the process of transformation.

Prayer

Father, I give myself to You as a love offering. You are my everything. You love me too much to leave me where I am. I lay myself down on your altar, Your "operating table", and I trust You to take me through the process of transformation. I know that You love me now just as I am, but I also want You to fulfill the dream that You have for my life, the very hope and future that You have planned for me. I give You my "yes". It's the very least that I can do in comparison to all You do for me. I trust You to finish what You have started and to keep me safe along the way. I choose to rest in Your love. Amen.

Faith Declaration

"God believes in me. He is *completely* committed to my success!"

Activation

- Make a fresh commitment today to be a student of God's Word.
- If your hunger has waned, you can simply ask right now for God to bring you back to that place of healthy hunger. He will!
- Ask God to show you those great and mighty things which you know not,[5] and *expect Him to do so* over the days ahead.
- Take a moment in prayer and picture a low point in your life, a time when you were floundering in your own mess. Forgive yourself. Ask Jesus to show you where He was in that memory and what He was doing. Watch and listen. Record the beautiful truths He reveals. (Do this as many times as needed for other low points in your past.)

ENDING HARMFUL CYCLES

The Way

*T*here is no formula to freedom, but there is a way to freedom. Jesus is the way. If we follow His way and surrender our own ways, we will find an abundant, beautiful life in His footsteps.

> "Jesus said to all of his followers, 'If you truly desire to be my disciple, you must disown your life completely, embrace my cross as your own, and surrender to my ways. For if you choose self-sacrifice, giving up your lives for my glory, you will embark on a discovery of more and more of true life. But if you choose to keep your lives for yourselves, you will lose what you try to keep.'"
>
> — LUKE 9:23-24, TPT

If we have harmful, sinful, and wasteful cycles in our lives, we have to ask, "Lord where have I put down my cross?" All sin was broken at the cross. It is because of the cross that we are free to make right choices. We are called and empowered to choose well.

> "...You should not live like the unbelievers around you who walk in their empty delusions. Their corrupted logic has been clouded because their hearts are so far from God—their blinded understanding and deep-seated moral darkness keeps them from the true knowledge of God. Because of spiritual apathy, they surrender their lives to lewdness, impurity, and sexual obsession. But this is not the way of life that Christ has unfolded within you. If you have really experienced the Anointed One, and heard his truth, it will be seen in your life; for we know that the ultimate reality is embodied in Jesus! And he has taught you to let go of the lifestyle of the ancient man, the old self-life, which was corrupted by sinful and deceitful desires that spring from delusions. Now it's time to be made new by every revelation that's been given to you. And to be transformed as you embrace the glorious Christ-within as your new life and live in union with him! For God has re-created you all over again in his perfect righteousness, and you now belong to him in the realm of true holiness."
>
> — EPHESIANS 4:17-24, TPT

Your Part

God has a part to do. You have a part to do. God will not do your part. It is helpful in understanding the function of the soul to view it as a processing center. Everything coming in through our senses is stored and processed here. It is like a filter for our entire being. Within this processing center is a huge storage bank consisting of all information that we have gathered, processed, and filed throughout our life experiences. This place of processing includes the conscious as well as the subconscious mind as previously discussed. It also includes the good and not so good information.

Our mind is truly amazing. The complexity of the brain is outstanding, and it is also *changeable.* It has fluidity in 3 important ways:

1. We can learn and grow.
2. We can self-regulate.
3. We can stop and/or change toxic thinking.

What does this tell us? *We can take charge of our mind, master our emotions, and mature in our decision making.* We may feel stuck, but the moment we say yes to God and align our will with His, all of heaven comes in and helps us, backing up our yes. Getting unstuck is just a right choice away because of what Jesus accomplished on Calvary!

As mentioned already, a critical fact that we need to understand as followers of Christ is that over 80% of the activity of our soul is taking place on a *subconscious* level. Why does that bear repeating?

We Live The Truth We Believe

Think of it like this. Let's say while growing up your mother was gone too often, and, when she was home, she was usually preoccupied and never seemed to be available when you needed her. Later in life, you perpetuate your childhood experience by not needing others. You love the people in your life but prefer to take care of yourself. In your heart (or subconscious mind) you have processed the information from your neglected childhood and believed the lie that you are safer and happier if you only depend on yourself for help and comfort. Consequently, your relationship with Holy Spirit, in particular, is distant and limited. He wants to be your comforter, but because of this lie, you don't know how to be comforted. You never learned how to let Him in.

From this example, we can see that it is *from our soul* that we live. That storage bank will make or break us and is either positively or negatively influencing *every decision* we make. This is why we must experience soul transformation. Otherwise, we will simply continue on in the same poor cycles perpetuated by the same wounds and lies that influence us in the thousands of choices we make daily.

The good news is that our souls can be renewed! In fact, that is God's strong recommendation to all believers.

"Stop imitating the ideals and opinions of the culture around you, but be inwardly transformed by the Holy Spirit through a total reformation of how you think. This will empower you to discern God's will as you live a beautiful life, satisfying and perfect in his eyes."

— ROMANS 12:2, TPT

Yes, this "beautiful life" that Paul spoke of is God's desire for you. He dreams and thinks beautiful thoughts about you and has wondrous plans for you, plans that are exceedingly, abundantly above your expectations (Ephesians 3:20). Your inward transformation is key. He knows it, we know it, and, let's be real, the enemy knows it, too.

God is Practical

God is mysterious, miraculous, and even mystical, but He is also quite practical! I love the awesomeness of His power, wonder, and majesty, but I am so very grateful as well for His *practical wisdom*. Sometimes we believers can leave out or ignore some practicalities in our lives, but we can't really get away with doing that for long. Eventually, the highs of spiritual ecstasy dissipate, and the rubber meets the road.

What am I saying? Well, to put it bluntly, we are not meant to live high. Jesus is not our quick fix; He is our friend. As with any friendship, there is a give and take, an ebb and flow, sacrifice, mutual edification, and partnership.

In a mature friendship, there is a phenomenon of *selflessness*. There is a place of such love, trust, and honor in which seasoned friends learn to reason together and truly act like friends. Our friend Jesus certainly loves and enjoys us in our immaturity, but He died for a bride, a partner. He longs for us to grow up.

"I was a wall, and my breasts were like towers; Then I became in his eyes as one who finds peace."

— Song of Solomon 8:10, NASB

The bride of Christ pictured here is equipped to feed and nurture others. She carries peace and therefore is able to provide strength and stability. She is a wall; she has no places of access for enemies, and so she is a shelter for others. In short, she is mature.

Jesus is awaiting our greater maturity, evidenced by great peace, in order to *partner* with us in a *greater* measure. He wants a bride who will put away childish ways and walk in mature love.[1] If maturity is going to be realized in us for Jesus's sake—for the sake of our Bride-groom—then we will of necessity have to *submit to the process* that will take us there.

The Process of Transformation

The process is practical! What does that mean? It's like this. I can love the smell of a clean home. I can love the sense of order and peace that it brings to my day and to my life. But no matter how much I *love* those results, I will never, ever enjoy them in my life if I don't submit to the process of housework! I love my teeth. I would like to take all of them with me to the grave. However, I will die toothless unless I submit to the practical wisdom and discipline of toothbrushing!

These are somewhat silly examples, but I believe the point is clear and very important. There are things we want in life (spiritually and naturally), but wanting is not enough. Even praying for those goals and dreams is not enough. Ultimately, no matter how gifted, dedicated, talented, or nurtured we are, we will never experience our dreams if we don't submit to the process of the practical, day to day (even moment to moment) decisions that will get us from point A to point B.

What does this have to do with soul transformation? It has every-thing to do with it. God can do anything, but there are some things He won't do. For those things He says to *us*, "Remember this truth: 'I can do all things through Christ who gives ME strength'" (Philip-pians 4:13).

Little by Little

Early on in my walk with Christ, I really viewed Him as my knight in shining armor. He was my champion, rescuer, and hero. Doesn't that sound good? It is good unless that is *all* He is. It was a painful chrysalis phase (remember the caterpillars) for me when I had to mature a bit in my faith in this area.

One particular time I was in prayer about an issue in my life. I prayed very specifically one day during my prayer time for Jesus to come in on a white horse and rescue me. I prayed fervently and with tears. I truly believed He could do anything, and I wanted Him to do *something*, but He didn't.

I had a dear friend who was a prayer warrior. I shared my need with her, and she faithfully prayed for me. After a day or two, she came to me and told me what God had shown her in prayer.

She said that it was really strange and that she hoped it wouldn't hurt my feelings. This was not what I wanted to hear! She lovingly told me that she prayed about my situation, but God interrupted her and told her to tell me that He was not going to come in on a white horse and rescue me. Whoa!

As you can imagine, this rocked my world. I was forced to let Jesus out of the little box that I had put Him in. I was also forced to put my big girl pants on and get a clue! God had done His part already; it was time for me to do my part (which He had already shown me). I now had a choice to make, a choice to take up my cross and follow or put my cross down and pout.

*God can do anything, but He loves us
too much to do our part for us.*

The Israelites in the wilderness with Moses faced this same decision over and over and over, and so do we. There has always been a cross to bear, and there always will be.

Sadly, we can be living a cross-less life, and no one around us may even notice, but God knows. In whatever area of our Christian walk we have put down our cross, we must go back, say yes to God, pick it back up, and move forward. Anything less is *powerless religiosity*.

God *has* planned victory for us though! Hand in hand with Him, little by little, we will drive out the enemies in the land.

> "The Lord your God will drive out those nations before you, little by little. You will not be allowed to eliminate them all at once, or the wild animals will multiply around you."
>
> — Deuteronomy 7:22, NIV

> "So don't be intimidated by them. GOD, your God, is among you — GOD majestic, GOD awesome. GOD, your God, will get rid of these nations, bit by bit. You won't be permitted to wipe them out all at once lest the wild animals take over and overwhelm you. But GOD, your God, will move them out of your way—he'll throw them into a huge panic until there's nothing left of them. He'll turn their kings over to you and you'll remove all trace of them under Heaven. Not one person will be able to stand up to you; you'll put an end to them all."
>
> — Deuteronomy 7:21-24, MSG

God has a master plan, and it's a good one! That plan pretty much moves along at the speed you allow it to.

God has a part. You have a part. He won't do your part. Obedience is the key, *and the gas pedal.*

The Master Plan

Can you picture your life on a continuum?

Picture in your mind your own precious timeline with key points along the way where divine moments of grace occurred, pulling you to God's heart and to your destiny.

Remember where and how you first heard the gospel. Picture your life at the moment you first felt His call in your heart, and you *knew* you needed a savior. Recall how completely lost you were, and yet He called you by name! Remember all the many, countless ways that He was working behind the scenes to bring you into your best moments, best choices, best relationships, and best places.

How obvious it is that He is *so* invested in your success! He is your champion and your biggest fan. He is truly the *best* lover of your soul. Further, He certainly hasn't brought you this far to leave you. In fact, He will never leave nor forsake you.

He will not abandon you in the process.

However, He will never settle for a codependent relationship with you. *You are much too important in His heart for that.* He doesn't want codependents; He wants co-laborers and friends. Yes, even a marriage partner.

"Let us rejoice and exalt him and give him glory, because the wedding celebration of the Lamb has come. And his bride has made herself ready."

— Revelations 19:7, TPT

For soul transformation and the renewing of our mind, the bride has some work to do. She must make herself ready! So, in part two we will discuss some very practical and simple (not necessarily easy) activities that will bring us into the maturity that will satisfy the heart of our Bridegroom while simultaneously creating the beautiful life we long for.

Summary

- I have a job to do in my soul transformation, and God won't do it.
- By God's Grace, I can take charge of my mind, master my emotions, and mature in my decision making.
- Jesus loves me in my immaturity, but He is waiting for a mature bride.
- God is increasing me little by little as I continue to obey and follow Him.
- I am required to carry my cross, just like Christ.
- God's plan for me is trustworthy and good.

Prayer

Dear God, thank You for being so patient and faithful to me during our journey together. Even when I couldn't understand all Your ways, I could trust Your heart. You always have my best in mind. Thank You for that. Help me to stay in the process and not to check out by being lukewarm. Help me take up my cross and follow You, even when it is hard. Help me to make a deeper commitment to You in the little decisions that I make every day. Amen.

Faith Declaration

"Jesus is my best friend. I choose to become a good friend to Him as well."

Activation

1. Take some time and ask God to show you any places in your walk where you have laid down your cross. Go back, say yes, take up your cross, and follow Him.
2. Ask the Lord to show you the one thing that you need to do right now in order to unlock future steps, blessings, and breakthroughs.
3. Picture Jesus as a bridegroom waiting for His bride. Ask Jesus how He feels about you, and then listen. Record what He reveals.

Some Interesting Facts About Butterflies

Egg:

- All the ingredients are there! Nothing is missing.
- Small and often unseen
- **Full of potential at this stage**

Larva (caterpillar):

- Furry, ugly, slimy - ew factor
- Belly crawler - lowly, humble, needy
- Hungry
- **Miraculous growth takes place in this stage.**

Pupa (chrysalis)

- Poopy stage
- Dark, alone, no nourishment
- Completely vulnerable, unprotected
- Seemingly dead
- **Miraculous transformation takes place at this stage.**

Imago (adult butterfly):

- Colorful and beautiful
- Can fly!
- **Able to reproduce at this stage, having reached full potential**

PART 2

UNVEILING JOURNEY — The Process of Transformation

Do you realize how much pleasure you bring the Lord? You are His delight, His pride and joy! We look at our weaknesses and want to hide, but Jesus sees us as we really are in Him; and He says, "But, you are so lovely!"[1]

At this point in your walk with God, you have blessed His heart by saying yes to His call to follow Him forward in your journey of transformation. He has so much He wants to show you and show forth in you...but it requires your cooperation. In this section, we will discover the ways in which we must cooperate with Him. Remember, He really does do the "heavy lifting" in this process, I promise. Just tuck yourself into His loving heart and continue saying yes. Your yes is lovely to Him, and it will take you all the way into your promised land of inheritance, peace, and blessing.

4

TWO TYPES OF WARFARE

Necessary or Unnecessary

*J*ust as there are many facets to God's character (Healer, Savior, Friend, Warrior, King, Comforter), there are also many facets to the life of a believer. We are simultaneously: a child of God, a friend of God, co-heirs with Christ, His bride, a minister of reconciliation, a disciple, a student of His Word, a preacher of the gospel, and so on. We are also warriors. I don't know about you, but I am thankful that I am not *only* a warrior.

If Christianity consisted only of warfare, that would not be nearly as much fun! I am glad that after I war, I can then come and just sit at His feet and rest in His love. But, we *are* warriors which means we must have a warrior mindset and a warrior heart. It also means we must be equipped and trained for war. God's Word is our manual and a powerful weapon.

"Your hand-to-hand combat is not with human beings, but with the highest principalities and authorities operating in rebellion under the heavenly realms. For they are a powerful class of demon-gods and evil spirits that hold this dark world in bondage."

— EPHESIANS 6:12, TPT

"For although we live in the natural realm, we don't wage a military campaign employing human weapons, using manipulation to achieve our aims. Instead, our spiritual weapons are energized with divine power to effectively dismantle the defenses behind which people hide."

— 2 CORINTHIANS 10:3-4, TPT

"...so that we would not be exploited by the adversary, Satan, for we know his clever schemes."

— 2 CORINTHIANS 2:11, TPT

"Be well balanced and always alert, because your enemy, the devil, roams around incessantly, like a roaring lion looking for its prey to devour."

— 1 PETER 5:8, TPT

"We can demolish every deceptive fantasy that opposes God and break through every arrogant attitude that is raised up in defiance of the true knowledge of God. We capture, like prisoners of war, every thought and insist that it bow in obedience to the Anointed One."

— 2 CORINTHIANS 10:5, TPT

"Put on God's complete set of armor provided for us, so that you will be protected as you fight against the evil strategies of the accuser."

— EPHESIANS 6:11, TPT

It is clear to me from just these few scriptures that being a Christian means we are engaged actively in an ongoing battle. We *do* wrestle. The problem, however, is that many times we are in the *wrong* wrestling match. Let me explain.

There are basically two types of warfare or two fights. One is *necessary* warfare, and one is what I like to refer to as *unnecessary warfare.*

Necessary warfare is normal. It is what we should expect to deal with on our journey with God as we advance! We are not ordinary! We are the army of the living God. We are blazing a path through this life, following the Lamb wherever He leads, and sharing His truth and power wherever we go.

> "And as you go, preach this message: 'Heaven's kingdom realm is accessible, close enough to touch.' You must continually bring healing to lepers and to those who are sick, and make it your habit to break off the demonic presence from people, and raise the dead back to life. Freely you have received the power of the kingdom, so freely release it to others. You won't need a lot of money."
>
> — MATTHEW 10:7-9, TPT

That's us! We are always being led in triumph. We are going from glory to glory! As we march, we should expect to have to put a smack-down on the devil along the way.

> "We are pressed but not crushed persecuted but not abandoned...Yet in all these things we are more than conquerors and gain an overwhelming victory through Him who loved us [so much that He died for us]."
>
> — ROMANS 8:37, AMP

Woohoo! This is the necessary warfare that we engage in as the Kingdom of God is forcefully advancing through us.

"From the moment John stepped onto the scene until now, the realm of heaven's kingdom is bursting forth, and passionate people have taken hold of its power."

— MATTHEW 11:12, TPT

Thirty-Eight Years

There is a New Testament story that gives us insight into taking hold of the Kingdom and our inheritance. In John chapter five, Jesus had a very interesting encounter. This is the familiar story of the man at the pool of Bethesda. The backdrop to the story is full of insight for us. The crippled man had been in a period of waiting. In his waiting, he likely had lost hope: hope in his healing, his future, his friends, his family (where were they?), and perhaps even God. After all, this was no ordinary wait. He had been in his crippled condition for thirty-eight, long years.

The number thirty-eight is significant in scripture. This is the same number of years that the children of Israel spend wandering in the desert before stepping into (taking hold of) their inheritance which was the promised land. During those years, they traveled around the wilderness, literally and figuratively going around the mountain, stuck in a defeating cycle.

"And the LORD spoke to me, saying, "You have circled this mountain long enough."

— DEUTERONOMY 2:2-3, NASB

Thirty-eight years speaks of passivity and unbelief. After those long years, what happened? Finally, the hearts of God's people had come to faith and into agreement with Him and His promises. This is true also for the man at the pool of Bethesda.

Bethesda means *house of lovingkindness*. This man is a picture of so many that are in the right place but are unable to "step in" to their promises, dreams, and sonship. The five porches at the pool speak of the Torah (five books of the law). He was under the law, and in that place he could not get healed, only hurt. But, just as is the case for each of us, his moment came. The living word, Jesus Christ, the true house of lovingkindness, came walking into his dilemma.

> "Now there was a man who had been disabled for thirty-eight years lying among the multitude of the sick. When Jesus saw him lying there, he knew that the man had been crippled for a long time. So Jesus said to him, 'Do you truly long to be healed?' The sick man answered him, 'Sir, there's no way I can get healed, for I have no one who will lower me into the water when the angel comes. As soon as I try to crawl to the edge of the pool, someone else jumps in ahead of me.' Then Jesus said to him, 'Stand up! Pick up your sleeping mat and you will walk!' Immediately he stood up—he was healed! So he rolled up his mat and walked again."
>
> —JOHN 5:5-9, TPT

Jesus asked him the important question, "Do you truly long to be healed?" The man's need was quite evident, but his faith and passion were not. Jesus came—love came—and inspired faith, hope, and love within his downhearted soul.

Isn't the Lord so good? The man, like us, was stuck in his cycle of hope-deferred and striving, but Jesus came to him! Thank God, He comes to us! Jesus came for him and for us to give us the amazing *choice* to rise up out of hopelessness, passivity, doubt, and unbelief and to cast off the past (thirty-eight years). Jesus invited the man to "Stand up, pick up your sleeping mat, and walk." This was his choice. It is ours as well. Friends, the House of Lovingkindness is our home, and we have all the benefits. The promised land is ours, but it will require the fighter in us to arise and step in.

But, it is also a fixed fight! Right? Because we know already that we have won. In fact, we are merely enforcing Christ's victory at

Calvary. He said that it is finished because it is! *He has won.* He won our victory, and He has all authority in heaven and earth. We have been given that same authority. We have authority over all the power of the devil. All means all. If we have all authority, that means the devil has none! Why then do we see defeat at times in the lives of believers? Is God's word not exact? Was Jesus speaking in hyperbole? Absolutely not!

> "He canceled out every legal violation we had on our record and the old arrest warrant that stood to indict us. He erased it all—our sins, our stained soul—he deleted it all and they cannot be retrieved! Everything we once were in Adam has been placed onto his cross and nailed permanently there as a public display of cancellation."
>
> — COLOSSIANS 2:14, TPT

What should we do then when our experience doesn't line up with the words of Christ? Sadly, this is when many will enter into doubt, fear, or unbelief. Hearts may harden at this point as disappointed or confused saints disbelieve God's truth and exchange it for a lie that they can live with. As a result, sin is tolerated, truth is minimized, victory over sin and Satan becomes a distant dream (someday, when I get to heaven), and the once passionate warrior bride is lulled to sleep.

Asleep But Not At Rest

> "This is why we must not fall asleep, as the rest do, but keep wide awake and clearheaded. For those who are asleep sleep the night away, and drunkards get drunk at night. But since we belong to the day, we must stay alert and clearheaded by placing the breastplate of faith and love over our hearts, and a helmet of the hope of salvation over our thoughts."
>
> — 1 THESSALONIANS 5:6-8, TPT

Ah, it is not a restful slumber. Not in the least. At this point, one battle has been traded for another. No longer are we going forth and conquering. Instead, we battle darkness *within* from an enemy that we have *allowed* to taunt us by giving him access to our "land." We are no longer advancing but rather are beating the air (so to speak), going in circles, and participating in *unnecessary warfare.*

Our *promised land* of a peaceful soul-life and garden of Eden intimacy with the Father has been *compromised.* Now, we find ourselves struggling in wrestling matches we can't win. Cycles of sin and defeat abound. We may even have to live a double life to keep secret the sins and fears that we feel powerless to stop.

It is this low-level living that made me desperate for freedom in my own life. I wanted more than what I was living. I believed God's word. I faithfully served God and His body. I tried *so* hard. The defeat in my life was not a result of lack of effort! In fact, I exhausted myself in my effort to live free.

How very sad that many Christians feel the same way I did. I didn't know that it wasn't meant to be so hard!

I had many well-meaning believers giving me advice. They told me to do this, do that, do *more* of this, do *more* of that, and so on. I also had the other extreme of friends telling me that it was all grace and that I needed to stop working. Actually, all of their counsel was true. But it wasn't the whole truth. I needed the full counsel of God.

God could see what neither myself nor my friends could see. He saw that the *cause* of my cycles of defeat were enemies in my life that had a *legal right* to be there. They had a *place* in my land. In certain areas of long-standing issues in my life, I was defeated from the *inside.*

An Inside Job

It's an inside job. We always need to remember that. When God frees us, it's an inside job. When the devil defeats us, it's an inside job. The key to victory is taking back forfeited territory.

We must determine, by the help of God, where we shook hands with the devil and granted him real estate in our soul.

There are basically five ways by which Satan gains entrance into a believer's life: disobedience, inner vows or judgments, curses, unforgiveness, and wounds. We will discuss these points of access in the next few chapters and take the steps required to close these doors to the enemy.

Summary

- There are basically two types of warfare Christians face: necessary (get into *this* battle) and unnecessary (get *out* of this battle).
- I am called to be a warrior and not a passive onlooker.
- If I have cycles of repeated defeat, it is likely that the enemy has legal ground in my life. God wants me to take that ground back.

Prayer

Father, I thank You that You have planned no defeat for me. Your plan is triumph! Reveal to me the areas of my life where I seem to be going "around the mountain" over and over again. I now commit those areas to You, and I ask You to help me take back my land from the enemy. I trust You to show me my path to victory.

Faith Declaration

"I am not meant for defeat. I am an overcomer!"

Activation

- Ask God to show you any area of your life where you have accepted defeat. Whether it is health, relationships, finances, or your future—take time to listen for what God reveals.
- Repent, and break those agreements.
- Now, over each specific area, release life. You can speak life by speaking the opposite of what you may see or what the enemy is saying. Partner with Heaven by saying what God is saying! (For example, "I have a bright future!" "My marriage is blessed by God!" "Healing is mine because of Christ's shed blood!")

ACCESS POINT 1: DISOBEDIENCE

*O*nce we have determined that the warfare we are engaged in is not victorious and advancing but rather cyclical and defeated, we are ready to partner with the Lord and kick out the enemies within our land.

Satan is a legalist. He has to operate legally. The story of Job actually perfectly illustrates this truth. Satan recognized he could not touch God's servant. He saw Job's hedge of protection and his righteousness. In fact, he had to come to the very throne of God to taunt and accuse God about Job.

> "One day when the angels came to report to God, Satan, who was the Designated Accuser, came along with them. God singled out Satan and said, 'What have you been up to?' Satan answered God, 'Going here and there, checking things out on earth.'
>
> GOD said to Satan, 'Have you noticed my friend Job? There's no one quite like him—honest and true to his word, totally devoted to God and hating evil.' Satan retorted, 'So do you think Job does all that out of the sheer goodness of his heart? Why, no one ever had

it so good! You pamper him like a pet, make sure nothing bad ever happens to him or his family or his possessions, bless everything he does—he can't lose!

But what do you think would happen if you reached down and took away everything that is his? He'd curse you right to your face, that's what.' GOD replied, 'We'll see. Go ahead—do what you want with all that is his. Just don't hurt him.' Then Satan left the presence of GOD."

—Job 1:6-12, MSG

There is so much rich revelation in this story about our walk with God, but one thing for certain is revealed.

Satan must have legal access into a person's life in order to torment them.

The first door of legal access that we will discuss is personal sin or disobedience.

Sin: Why Do We Do It?

Often, sin is our attempt to meet a valid need in a wrong way. We are not mechanical, unfeeling, inhuman robots. We are wonderful, vibrant, God-designed, human beings created in God's image with real, basic human needs such as nourishment, shelter, love, fellowship, exhilaration, rest, protection, healing, self-worth, identity, protection, provision, consolation, comfort, and companionship.

We have a loving, strong, protective, and generous heavenly Father. In Jesus, we have a brother, friend, and lover. Lastly, we have a comforter, guide, and teacher in the person of Holy Spirit.

He is *El Shaddai*, the All-Sufficient One, who is well able to satisfy us.

He delights in us and delights in meeting every need we have. That is His grand design! He *is* the great I Am. He is the answer for every need we have. He is fully capable of being our all in all. But, we have to choose to let Him meet our needs. When we attempt to satisfy our needs outside of God, sin is the result. Sin may satisfy momentarily, hence the pleasures of sin for a season referenced in Hebrews 11:25, but the payback is not worth the momentary relief or pleasure we experience. The reward, fruit, and wages of sin in our lives is death.[1]

It is also important to recognize the fact that simply ignoring or suppressing needs doesn't work either. Our needs are real, and no matter how human or fleshly we may think them, they are not evil desires. We can't just shut down or ignore our needs.

Take for example the need for rest. Unless God gives us permission to go against natural laws, we need seven to eight hours of sleep per day, as well as sabbath rests. Ignoring this need doesn't show our stamina but rather our foolish pride. Eventually, an ignored need will cause a malfunction somewhere in our lives. It is in fact an open door to our cunning enemy who is always seeking opportunity to infiltrate our defenses.

This is a small example, but the principle can be applied to *every* need we have in our humanity: comfort, companionship, shelter, hunger, recreation, intimacy, and more. So, all that to say, needs cannot be stuffed away. They must be met.

When we have a need, we basically have three options as to how to have that need met.

1. We can bring it to God and let Him fill it.
2. We can attempt to meet the need on our own, in our flesh and in our own strength.
3. We can choose to accept Satan's counterfeit, or substitute, to fill our need.

The Bible says in James that when we sin, we should not say we are tempted by God. Rather, *we put ourselves* in the position to be tempted by Satan when we allow ourselves to be drawn away by *our own lust*.

Lust is the byproduct of meeting a need outside of God. We settle for a false comfort in place of the true comforter (some examples include gluttony, pornography, chronic worry, unhealthy soul-ties, etc.), and because these cannot *truly* meet the need, a cycle is created in us of repeating the sinful activity in order to get the temporary relief or fix again and again and again.

This is called spiritual slavery or bondage, and it is Satan's plan for us all. However, God says this:

> "Let me be clear, the Anointed One has set us free—not partially, but completely and wonderfully free! We must always cherish this truth and stubbornly refuse to go back into the bondage of our past."
>
> — GALATIANS 5:1, TPT

This is where we have to get *real* with ourselves and with God about our issues.

All sin leads to bondage if we don't repent.

We will discuss repentance later. First, let's park on this topic of slavery. If we are indeed obeying a master other than Christ, we are in the snare of the enemy and in danger of being drawn further and further from God's heart.

In the beautiful story of the prodigal son we often assume that the travesty was in the fact that a son was reduced to the pigpen, but I really feel that *anywhere outside of the Father's embrace is a pigpen.* Wasn't the elder brother in the story in a bit of a pigpen himself? Religious pride and jealousy is pretty stinky if you ask me.

We are meant for intimacy. *Anything less than intimacy with the father is low-level (pig-pen) living.* This is not the life Jesus died to give us. Chains of confusion, guilt, and shame are not His will for us. His plan and His Kingdom is righteousness, peace, and joy in the Holy Spirit. Even though our indiscretion or our sin may seem insignificant and hardly comparable to the prodigal son's pigpen, if we have left the father's bosom, we are surely just as much in the pigpen as the gravest sinner. What else would we call a fit of rage in comparison to accepting Father's protection? What is sexual sin compared to walking with God in the garden of fellowship in the cool of the evening? These poor substitutes look like pig slop next to His loveliness. He wants so much more for His beloved. His plan for us is peace and blessing.

So, we now know our needs are not good, bad, or ugly; they just are simply needs. Needs that are *opportunities* for hugs and kisses from Jesus, comfort and help from Holy Spirit, and great adventures with Daddy God. Getting your needs met by God provides opportunities for God Himself to meet with us and feast with us. He longs to give us personal encounters with Him that will not only satisfy our souls but also lead us into deeper intimacy and understanding of Him. These are the very things we truly need and want most. This is what our heart longs for!

Satisfaction Guaranteed

God is not merely trying to take away things or pleasures from us. He is wanting to *reveal* to us the pleasures of walking with Him. If He takes something out of our hands, it is only because He desires to fill them with something *far* better.

If we can see areas or even one area where needs have been met in an unhealthy way, it is simply time to repent and go back to the

Father's house! He hasn't left us. He is right where we left Him, and He is longing for our return. He is not angry, but He is grieving. Go back home, and change His sadness to joy.

Heaven will have a big party! The next thing you know, you'll find yourself covered again in your beautiful robe of righteousness, enjoying the peace that results from right standing with God, and having your joy of salvation fully and completely restored. *You were created for the Father's house!* You may feel you have squandered everything, but His love and grace toward you are *without bounds.* He will never stop being your dad no matter how you may have blown it. He will never change His mind about you!

Sin: What Does God Think of It?

God looked through eternal perspective before the foundations of the world, assessed the sin problem, and settled on the solution:

> "This is love: He loved us long before we loved him. It was his love, not ours. He proved it by sending his Son to be the pleasing sacrificial offering to take away our sins."
>
> — 1 JOHN 4:10, TPT

Even though He was perfect and sinless, beautifully pure, He became sin so that we could be clean and right before God.[2] So, just who are you? A sinner? No, let's not insult Jesus's beautiful accomplishment at Calvary like that! You are the very righteousness of God. Paul the apostle said it like this:

> "What a terrible thought! We have died to sin once and for all, as a dead man passes away from this life. So how could we live under sin's rule a moment longer?"
>
> — ROMANS 6:2 TPT

Turn to God. *You are free* to repent for sins and evil desires to which you have given yourself. Ask the Lord to show you what need you were trying to meet outside of Him, and then ask Him to meet that need for you. Ask Him to free you from all demonic powers you allowed access into your life through those sins, and He will break *every* chain of bondage and slavery!

You can be free from sin and become a slave to righteousness because Jesus said, "It is finished!"

I had a dear friend who, for a period of time, got herself trapped in the sin of homosexuality. She and I discussed her dilemma, and I tried to help her see God's truth and His heart for her in this situation. It was a tough conversation. It was difficult mainly because her path away from the Father's house was paved with a very deceptive lie of Satan. Her sticking point was that she had prayed and asked for God to take her wrong feelings away, but He didn't.

She had found a way to escape blame by shifting it onto God. *He didn't stop her from sinning.* This may sound ridiculous, but it is a fairly common deception. Adam and Eve utilized it quite well in the garden.

However, blame shifting doesn't alleviate guilt. Only forgiveness and repentance can erase guilt. To receive that blessed relief and freedom, we have to own our bad behavior and agree with the very important truth that sin—all sin—was completely defeated at the cross. It still is.

Remember, it's not about shame or fear. The problem of sin has already been remedied! *The real issue is whether or not this activity, this sin, hurts my relationship with God?* Sin always separates. That is the real issue.

Heart Idols

I knew a young man once who had gotten saved while in juvenile hall. Our church sent a ministry team there on a regular basis to minister to these young people, and his salvation was a wonderful result! He began attending our church and began to thrive. I will never forget listening to him share some of his testimony.

Many times (most times) when people share their story, they will tell of their misery in their sinful condition. They will share how very low and destructive their lives had become before Jesus rescued them. That was not his story!

Surprisingly, he said that he was having a blast in his sin! He loved his sin. He hadn't hit the "rock bottom" yet that many of us have to get to before we surrender. Sin was still mighty pleasurable to this young man. And yet, he gave it all up once he experienced the amazing love of God.

I share this story because I want to make an important point. Sometimes the sin that may be so easily besetting us does not seem so terrible. Therefore, it is very easy to reason away the voice of the Holy Spirit in our hearts urging us to let go of it.

In the story of that young man his fun sin was plainly anti-biblical. He was involved in drugs, sexual sin, bad influences, and more. Sometimes it's not so clear cut. *For those situations we simply choose what brings us closer to His heart.*

We choose what will promote our intimate relationship with Jesus.

We must not ignore His still small voice whispering to our hearts. He knows the idols in our hearts much better than we do. He knows very well what will turn our hearts aside and lead us to taking "luke-warm exit" in our journey with Him. He wants us hot, on fire for Him.

Take, for example, this familiar story of the rich young ruler:

> "As Jesus started on his way, a man came running up to him. Kneeling down in front of him, he cried out, 'Good Teacher, what one thing am I required to do to gain eternal life?' Jesus responded, 'Why do you call me good? Only God is truly good. You already know the commandments: 'Do not murder, do not commit adultery, do not steal, do not give a false testimony, do not cheat, and honor your father and mother.' The man said to Jesus, 'Teacher, I have carefully obeyed these laws since my youth.' Jesus fixed his gaze upon the man, with tender love, and said to him, 'Yet there is still one thing in you lacking. Go, sell all that you have and give the money to the poor. Then all of your treasure will be in heaven. After you've done this, come back and walk with me.' Completely shocked by Jesus' answer, he turned and walked away very sad, for he was extremely rich."
>
> — Mark 10:17-22, TPT

The "one thing" keeping this young man from the relationship with God that he desired was his wealth. Is it wrong to have wealth? No, many of the greatest people in scripture were rich. So then how could Jesus tell him that the one thing he lacked was surrendering his riches?

Very simple—it was the idol of his heart. He looked into the beautiful face of Jesus that day, asked the burning question of his soul, got his answer (which he probably already sensed deep inside), and then went away sad. He wasn't ready to surrender all.

For each of us, there will probably also be a "one thing." We won't be able to necessarily quote chapter and verse of why it's wrong. We may not necessarily be able to explain it well to others or even to ourselves, but it will make total sense to our hearts. Where it matters.

An undivided heart is key to deeper intimacy with God. If you find yourself wrestling with the Holy Spirit over something in your life, just let go. When you do, great peace will come! And you will feel the pleasure of God so greatly it may take your breath away...and His.

"Every part of you is so beautiful, my darling. Perfect is your beauty, without flaw within. Now you are ready, my bride, to come with me as we climb the highest peaks together. Come with me through the archway of trust. We will look down from the crest of the glistening mounts and from the summit of our sublime sanctuary. Together we will wage war in the lion's den and the leopard's lair as they watch nightly for their prey. For you reach into my heart. With one flash of your eyes I am undone by your love, my beloved, my equal, my bride. You leave me breathless— I am overcome by merely a glance from your worshiping eyes, for you have stolen my heart. I am held hostage by your love and by the graces of righteousness shining upon you. How satisfying to me, my equal, my bride. Your love is my finest wine—intoxicating and thrilling. And your sweet, perfumed praises—so exotic, so pleasing. Your loving words are like the honeycomb to me; your tongue releases milk and honey, for I find the Promised Land flowing within you. The fragrance of your worshiping love surrounds you with scented robes of white. My darling bride, my private paradise, fastened to my heart. A secret spring are you that no one else can have— my bubbling fountain hidden from public view. What a perfect partner to me now that I have you. Your life flows into mine, pure as a garden spring. A well of living water springs up from within you, like a mountain brook flowing into my heart!"

— SONG OF SONGS 4:7-12, 15, TPT

Lots of symbolism here (obviously), but *we need to see what is at stake!* If we hold on to some worthless heart idol, we are passing up on something so beautiful—the ability to captivate God's heart. Our undivided heart, our single eye of pure devotion, our choice for Him above all else, steals His heart and leaves Him breathless. Wow.

Things become clear and so much simpler when we just let go and surrender.

> "Then he [Jesus] told them what they could expect for themselves: 'Anyone who intends to come with me has to let me lead. You're not in the driver's seat—I am. Don't run from suffering; embrace it. Follow me and I'll show you how. Self-help is no help at all. Self-sacrifice is the way, my way, to finding yourself, your true self. What good would it do to get everything you want and lose you, the real you? If any of you is embarrassed with me and the way I'm leading you, know that the Son of Man will be far more embarrassed with you when he arrives in all his splendor in company with the Father and the holy angels. This isn't, you realize, pie in the sky by and by. Some who have taken their stand right here are going to see it happen, see with their own eyes the kingdom of God.'"
>
> — LUKE 9:23-27, MSG

> "For whosoever will save his life shall lose it: but whosoever will lose his life for my sake, the same shall save it."
>
> — LUKE 9:2, 4, KJV

Lay It All Down

The life we seek, the life our spirits long for, the *zoe* life of God (*real life*) is found at the place of complete surrender to Christ. We will always be wandering in the wilderness, just like the children of Israel, until we come to that place.

Shut the door of disobedience—right in the face of the devil. Be radical in your love for Jesus, knowing you only have one life to live out your devotion. Choose Jesus. He has already made His choice—He chose you.

Under the old covenant, God's people had to wait longingly for the year of Jubilee. Coming only every fifty years, it was literally a once in a lifetime opportunity. This was a time when debts were forgiven and slaves were set free. It didn't make sense. It wasn't fair. It was just a sovereign mandate from Heaven. Now today, even at this very moment (we don't have to wait) Jesus *is* our Jubilee! He is the way and has made a way for us to walk in complete victory and freedom. Why wait? Receive your Jubilee! Freedom is yours in Christ.

Here is a powerful passage the Apostle Paul wrote for us concerning victory over sin. It is full of transforming truth.

> "What shall we say, then? Shall we go on sinning so that grace may increase? By no means! We are those who have died to sin; how can we live in it any longer? Or don't you know that all of us who were baptized into Christ Jesus were baptized into his death? We were therefore buried with him through baptism into death in order that, just as Christ was raised from the dead through the glory of the Father, we too may live a new life.

> "For if we have been united with him in a death like his, we will certainly also be united with him in a resurrection like his. For we know that our old self was crucified with him so that the body ruled by sin might be done away with, that we should no longer be slaves to sin—because anyone who has died has been set free from sin.

> Now if we died with Christ, we believe that we will also live with him. For we know that since Christ was raised from the dead, he cannot die again; death no longer has mastery over him. The death he died, he died to sin once for all; but the life he lives, he lives to God.

In the same way, count yourselves dead to sin but alive to God in Christ Jesus. Therefore do not let sin reign in your mortal body so that you obey its evil desires. Do not offer any part of yourself to sin as an instrument of wickedness, but rather offer yourselves to God as those who have been brought from death to life; and offer every part of yourself to him as an instrument of righteousness. For sin shall no longer be your master, because you are not under the law, but under grace.

What then? Shall we sin because we are not under the law but under grace? By no means! Don't you know that when you offer yourselves to someone as obedient slaves, you are slaves of the one you obey—whether you are slaves to sin, which leads to death, or to obedience, which leads to righteousness? But thanks be to God that, though you used to be slaves to sin, you have come to obey from your heart the pattern of teaching that has now claimed your allegiance. You have been set free from sin and have become slaves to righteousness.

I am using an example from everyday life because of your human limitations. Just as you used to offer yourselves as slaves to impurity and to ever-increasing wickedness, so now offer yourselves as slaves to righteousness leading to holiness. When you were slaves to sin, you were free from the control of righteousness. What benefit did you reap at that time from the things you are now ashamed of? Those things result in death! But now that you have been set free from sin and have become slaves of God, the benefit you reap leads to holiness, and the result is eternal life. For the wages of sin is death, but the gift of God is eternal life in Christ Jesus our Lord."

— Romans 6:1-23, TPT

Summary

- Satan is a legalist and can only occupy an area of our life that he has legal access to.
- Satan is always seeking an access point in our lives.
- Disobedience is one way that we can give the enemy access.
- Sin is often the result of trying to meet a valid need in a wrong way.
- God wants our needs met, not ignored; we can trust Him to meet our needs.
- Sin is a fruit not a root. The real question is, *"What need was I trying to meet in an unholy way?"*

Prayer

Father, I thank You that I don't need to run from You when I have sinned because You love me and want me close to Your heart. I recognize that all of my needs must be met. I repent of any way I have tried to meet my needs outside of Your will. Help me to stay within the healthy boundaries of Your Word and trust You to meet all my daily needs. Amen.

Faith Declaration

"I am holy unto the Lord. My life is not my own. I have been bought with a high price. I belong to Jesus!"

Activation

- Ask God to show you any needs you are trying to meet in an inordinate way.

- Present that need to Him, and ask Him to meet it.

- Repent of the sin you participated in, and ask God to

deliver you from demonic spirits you may have partnered with through these activities.

- Here is a good sample prayer:

I renounce Satan and all of his evil works. I renounce the works of my own flesh. Father, I repent of all my sins, and I ask for Your forgiveness. On the basis of Jesus's shed blood, I receive Your forgiveness and total freedom from sin. In Jesus's name, Amen.

ACCESS POINT 2: WOUNDS

"Jesus said to them, 'Listen. No one is able to break into a mighty man's house and steal his property unless he first overpowers the mighty man and ties him up. Then his entire house can be plundered and his possessions taken."

— Mark 3:27, TPT

"And I pray that he would unveil within you the unlimited riches of his glory and favor until supernatural strength floods your innermost being with his divine might and explosive power. Then, by constantly using your faith, the life of Christ will be released deep inside you, and the resting place of his love will become the very source and root of your life. Then you will be empowered to discover what every holy one experiences—the great magnitude of the astonishing love of Christ in all its dimensions. How deeply intimate and far-reaching is his love! How enduring and inclusive it is! Endless love beyond measurement that transcends our understanding—this extravagant love pours into you until you are filled to overflowing with the fullness of God!"

— Ephesians 3:16-19, TPT

It's An Inside Job

*T*he truths (or possibly lies that have become our perceived truth) that influence our conscious mind—including our emotions and decisions—come from what we have stored inside on our hard drive on a subconscious level. It directs us inherently, intuitively. It tells us to fear even when there seems to be no rational reason to fear. It tells us to be ashamed of ourselves even when we are cleared by Christ's blood. When we have committed no wrong, it screams at us that *we are wrong*. It overrides the precious imago whispered to our hearts from God's mouth and attempts to overshadow who we truly are.

How does our subconscious mind get its information? This is a big subject (just ask Freud), but for the sake of our study of healing and freedom, we will discuss a few key sources.

Unhealed Childhood Memories and Traumatic Experiences

I have had the opportunity to be a part of many prayer ministry times as God brought healing to memories in people's souls. It is common for God to go all the way back even to infant and toddler experiences in a person's life to heal trauma and expose lies that were believed at a very early stage of human development. Young children are not equipped to analyze what they experience, so, many times, they just internalize it. Negative or harmful experiences lead to distortions and dysfunctions becoming hard wired into them as normal. It becomes part of their 80% storage bank, and they never even make the conscious decision to put it there! It just happens.

Some children that go through trauma learn that it is normal to feel:

- alone
- abused
- stressed

- unwanted
- lack
- neglected
- fearful
- Etc.

That is their normal. Therefore, peace does not feel right or normal. Being loved and accepted does not feel right. Having more than enough does not feel right. Can you see how these lies and wounds can set them up for a difficult adulthood?

I have a dear friend who has no memory of ever being held as a child. He does however distinctly remember the day his father left him at the age of three. He remembers being told by his mother that he was ugly, and he remembers being told that he was just like his father. What was his normal? Being unwanted, and as a result, he worked very hard at his poor attitudes and delinquent behavior throughout his teen years to earn rejection. People's responses to his bad behavior seemed to prove that he was indeed unwanted. But God. God proved His faithful love to him and healed his broken heart, and we've been married now for over twenty-seven years!

We can actually even open doors for the enemy to influence unborn babies through our judgments and actions against them. I remember, when I became pregnant with our fourth child, I was not ready to be pregnant. I thought I was done having babies. I wasn't so good at being pregnant! I am one of those ladies that is sick for the whole nine months. Now, pregnant again, I had three small children to care for when all I felt like doing was to lay on the couch, fighting nausea. During the first few weeks of my misery, unknowingly, without an intentional thought to do harm, I rejected my baby. I just simply didn't want to be pregnant.

I am *so* thankful that God swooped into my situation to show me what I had done! I myself had dealt with a familiar spirit of rejection in my own life, and God revealed to me that the enemy was attempting to perpetuate the same sin in the life of my child. I immediately repented and broke rejection off my baby. I declared and decreed over her that she was *wanted*, that she had a great destiny, and that she was a vital, blessed, and welcomed member of our family.

When she was born, we named her Promise! What a huge blessing she is in so many ways. I cannot even imagine our family without Promise, but I truly believe that if I had not repented and broken that rejection, she would have been born with and maintained a sense of rejection over her life. She could have lived a life expecting rejection and even tempting others to reject her over and over as a cycle of rejection. It was an assignment of the enemy, but it was thwarted!

Satan Targets Children

I have heard it taught that the enemy has a well thought out plan for us from the moment we are conceived. He is quite patient also. It is important that we are not flippant about our enemy. He is certainly not flippant about us!

Please don't misunderstand me. I am not exalting him or his works. He is a defeated foe. *But he is a foe, and he is crafty.* He starts working against our destinies in God early so that he can try to sabotage our connection to the Godhead (our Heavenly Father, our Lord Jesus, and our teacher and comforter Holy Spirit). In short, his agenda is to mar our image of ourselves and of God.

One story comes to mind that illustrates this point. A man was receiving inner healing ministry, and during one particular prayer session, the Lord took him to a memory where he saw himself in a bouncy seat as an infant. There was a lot of activity going on around him by the adults in his life, but he was being ignored. He saw himself in that memory and felt how alone he was. When he asked Jesus where He was in that past moment, Jesus came over to the baby and picked him up and just held him. The truth (the *real* truth) was that he wasn't alone. He was never alone. God healed that wound in his soul and subsequent lonely memories that escalated that lie of aloneness throughout his life. The healing work God can do to our soul is so awesome.

One notable thing about this was that the man in this story had issues later in his life (before his healing) with being unhealthily independent. He usually felt that he was on his own even as a committed Christian. He knew from scripture that God was his father and friend, but in his heart, he maintained a *profound sense of aloneness*. He felt a deep need to do things for himself so as not to depend on others and, even on some levels, God. The truth in his head did not match the truth in his heart. As a result he did not have *peace* in this area of his soul.

How wonderful that God knows exactly where we need to be healed! He has so much compassion over us because He knows *why* we do what we do. He understands, and He *so* wants to remove the lies that influence us and show us the truth that frees us!

> "Stop imitating the ideals and opinions of the culture around you, but be inwardly transformed by the Holy Spirit through a total reformation of how you think. This will empower you to discern God's will as you live a beautiful life, satisfying and perfect in his eyes."
>
> — Romans 12:2, TPT

This is one way in which our souls get rewired and our minds renewed. We call it healing memories, but I realize this may sound a bit mystical to some. What is actually taking place in this healing is that lies that were believed during past traumatic moments are exposed and reconciled to the truth.

When this wonderful miracle takes place, we get unlocked, spiritually. The truth actually sets us free. Memories, as well as all thoughts, take up space in our brain. They are real parts of our soul that can be healthy or toxic. If they are toxic, they affect our mental health (and subsequently our physical and spiritual health), but they can be healed! God is our healer. He longs to heal us in spirit, mind, and body.

You can experience this on your own in your personal prayer time with the Lord. He can take you to memories that need to be healed. He can expose lies that have been made false truths. I have provided some activations in this book to facilitate you in that process. However, *I also want to strongly encourage everyone who reads this to find a ministry of inner healing where you can receive prayer and powerful help toward your freedom.* It is a good thing!

Inner Healing

One of my most amazing inner healing encounters was one in which I saw myself lift my heart up to Father God. It was beating, but broken. I saw Him sew it together like a physician making stitches. He literally bound up my broken heart. I had this experience after several weeks of spending time soaking in His presence and receiving ministry for inner healing and deliverance. It was a very significant time in my life. After this encounter, I felt different. I can't explain it other than to say a pain in my soul that had *always* been there was gone. It was healed.

"He heals the brokenhearted and binds up their wounds."

— Psalms 147:3, NIV

"He heals the wounds of every shattered heart."

— Psalms 147:3, TPT

I will share another story that illustrates the exposing of hidden lies and getting healed from the inside out. This is from my own life as well. I was actually by myself in prayer, and I was asking God to show me things that He wanted me to do for Him. I was asking Him for my next assignments. As I was praying, this feeling of mild anxiety kept rising up in me. I ignored it and just kept patiently waiting on the Lord for direction.

Finally, I realized that this anxious feeling was there, nagging me. Guess what? It was *frequently* there. It was so familiar and normal to me that I didn't even notice it most of the time. I had just learned to live with it like a low grade fever, like a symptom of an underlying ailment that I overlooked all the time. God was wanting to deal with it! He wanted me free. He wanted me (and you, too) to be able to move forward unafraid.

Once I clued in, I asked the Lord, "Where did this sense of anxiety concerning hearing and obeying Your will come from?" I didn't hear words from the Lord but instead got an instant download of the root cause of the fear. He showed me that in my early walk with Him, I had received some poor teaching about obeying God's voice. It wasn't false teaching, just not great teaching. It had left me with insecurity about my ability to please the Lord in that area. Could I hear Him clearly? Could I obey Him correctly? I wasn't *totally* sure, hence the nagging anxiety. Also, I had had some bad experiences that compounded the fear. When stepping out to obey God, I had experienced some painful failures. Lies had gotten into my heart in this area.

When He showed me the root, I released forgiveness to any person involved (mainly the teachers). I also renounced the lie that said I needed to fear "missing God," and I repented of partnering with the fear of failure along with other fears. I then asked the Lord to show me the truth.

Immediately, I saw a mental picture of myself in a huge office with many cubicles filling it. I had a cubicle, and I was sitting at my desk. I knew Father God was my boss! He came walking down the aisle toward my work area and almost carelessly tossed a file folder on my desk. I knew it was my assignment. I picked it up.

Afterwards, I asked the Lord what truth He wanted me to know about Him being my boss, and He told me three words that changed my outlook on serving Him forever. He simply said to me,

"I trust you." That has become my truth. He trusts me. If God believes in me, then I can believe in me, too!

Listen, God knows the good work that He has done in my life and in yours! *And He is pleased with it.* Ultimately, His pleasure in us is all that matters.

We are meant to walk in the sense of God's pleasure, not the fear of disappointing Him.

Look at these beautiful verses that teach the truth about obeying and following God:

> "For you bring me a continual revelation of resurrection life, the path to the bliss that brings me face-to-face with you."
>
> — PSALMS 16:11, TPT

> "To know you is to experience a flowing fountain, drinking in your life, springing up to satisfy. In your light we receive the light of revelation."
>
> — PSALMS 36:9, TPT

> "Her (wisdom's) ways are pleasant ways And all her paths are peace."
>
> — PROVERBS 3:17, NASB

> "So you'll go out in joy, you'll be led into a whole and complete life. The mountains and hills will lead the parade, bursting with song. All the trees of the forest will join the procession, exuberant with applause. No more thistles, but giant sequoias, no more thorn

bushes, but stately pines— Monuments to me, to GOD, living and lasting evidence of GOD."

— Isaiah 55:12-13, MSG

"No more thistles" and "no more thorns"—that is your destiny in God.

In whatever area of our lives we are not experiencing God's abundant peace—that is an area He wants to heal and free us.

The lack of peace that we may at times sense is the clue, the "low grade fever", the caution light on the dashboard of our soul that says, "Fix me, Jesus!" The good news, the very best news, is that He can and He will!

Oh, Yes, He Can!

"A man spoke up out of the crowd. 'Teacher,' he said, 'I have a son possessed by a demon that makes him mute. I brought him here to you, Jesus. Whenever the demon takes control of him, it knocks him down, and he foams at the mouth and gnashes his teeth, and his body becomes stiff as a board. I brought him to your disciples, hoping they could deliver him, but they were not strong enough.' Jesus said to the crowd, 'Why are you such a faithless people? How much longer must I remain with you and put up with your unbelief? Now, bring the boy to me.' So they brought him to Jesus. As soon as the demon saw him, it threw the boy into convulsions. He fell to the ground, rolling around and foaming at the mouth. Jesus turned to the father and asked, 'How long has your son been tormented like this?' 'Since childhood,' he replied. 'It tries over and over to kill him by throwing him into fire or water. But please, if you're able to do something, anything—have compassion on us and help us!' Jesus said to him, 'What do you mean 'if'? If you are able to believe, all things are possible to the believer.' When he heard this, the boy's father cried out with tears, saying, 'I do believe, Lord; help my little faith!' Now when Jesus saw that the crowd was quickly growing larger, he commanded the demon, saying, 'Deaf and mute spirit, I command you to come out of him and never enter him again!' The demon shrieked and threw the boy into terrible seizures and finally came out of him! As the boy lay there, looking like a corpse, everyone thought he was dead. But Jesus stooped down, gently took his hand, and raised him up to his feet, and he stood there completely set free! Afterwards, when Jesus arrived at the house, his disciples asked him in private, 'Why couldn't we cast out the demon?' He answered them, 'This type of powerful spirit can only be cast out by fasting and prayer.'"

— MARK 9:17-29, TPT

We are "the living and lasting evidence of God" (Isaiah 55:13). His goodness, love, power, and His *reality* are realized through our transformed lives and displayed to those around us who need to see just how good He is.

Summary

- The enemy works methodically and patiently to plant lies in our hearts.
- The enemy gains access through traumas and wounds that are unhealed, often planting lies there.
- Any area where we have lost hope is an area where a lie is operating.
- God is a master healer, the great physician of our souls. He

knows the wounds in our hearts and is well able to fix our brokenness.

- Healing occurs when God's truth displaces the lies. The truth makes us free!

Prayer

Father, You know every hurt, every unhealed wound, and every lie in my soul. I ask You to heal me completely. I give You permission to do this "spiritual surgery" in Your own way, in Your own timing, and with Your own tools. I know You can. I receive my healing now by faith which I know pleases You greatly. I thank You in advance for every touch, every encounter, and every blessing in my healing journey. Amen.

Faith Declaration

"Jesus will heal every hurt in my heart."

Activation

- Set aside some uninterrupted time alone with God (and bring some tissue).

- Ask the Lord to take you to a memory that He wants to heal. Let Him pick.

- Whatever memory comes to your mind and heart, focus on it. Sometimes people will say that they're just seeing flashes of lots of memories, or perhaps that they are just seeing a certain *time* or season in their life. That is just fine. Don't fret over picking the wrong memory. Just settle on one and trust God's tender guidance.

- Look around the memory, and see who you need to forgive. Forgive them out loud by name, and release them to God.

- Ask Him, "Lord when this happened in my life, what was the lie that I believed?"

- Ask, "Lord, what is the truth about that?"

- Finally, look around the memory and see where Jesus was. See what He is doing and hear what He may say.

- Go through this process as many times as feels necessary. Remember, this is your tool now! Take it out and use it when God reveals a traumatic past experience or memory that is unhealed. Follow His peace, and when your peace is interrupted, pay attention! God is showing you so that He can help you to wholeness.

ACCESS POINT 3: UNFORGIVENESS

Overcoming People Problems and Offense

I have heard it said that we are most like God when we forgive. I definitely see the truth of that, and it makes me think about the amazing forgiveness that God freely bestows on us. It so reveals His heart of gracious love. He is so merciful and kind, and scripture teaches us that He keeps no record of wrongs. His anger lasts a moment, but His favor goes on for a thousand generations--in other words, *forever*!

We have that same spirit living inside of us! We are endued with power from on high. We have His grace working within us to forgive *supernaturally*.

Being born into this world guarantees that we will have *many* opportunities to forgive. In order to navigate through what sometimes seems like a minefield of offenses, we must guard our hearts from the *prison* of unforgiveness. We have all spent some time in this particular prison cell. Maybe you find yourself there now. Let's take a few moments and see God's wisdom for us.

The New Command

We often hear of the great commandment to love God completely and love your neighbor as yourself, but there is actually a subsequent command; a higher law.

> "So I give you now a new commandment: Love each other just as much as I have loved you. For when you demonstrate the same love I have for you by loving one another, everyone will know that you're my true followers."
>
> —JOHN 13:34, TPT

The original command was love others as you love yourself, but Jesus takes it to the fullness—Love like He loves.

God is calling us to love others the way He has loved us.

Wow.

Just take a moment and think of how generous He has been in forgiving you. That is the way He wants us to deal with others. No. Matter. What. Even up to 70 x 7 times.[1]

So what do we do if we find ourselves still battling feelings of anger, resentment, and bitterness towards those who have wronged us or hurt us? I believe there is a key for us in this verse:

> "In this same way, my heavenly Father will deal with any of you if you do not release forgiveness from your heart toward your fellow believer."
>
> — MATTHEW 18:35, TPT

This entire passage is Jesus's great teaching on forgiveness (please read it all), but I want to focus on the phrase "from your heart."

From Your Heart

This phrase may frustrate you if you have been *trying* to forgive. Maybe it seems unattainable because the offense in your life is so very great. Part of the problem, I believe, is a misunderstanding of its meaning! Jesus was *not* saying, "Hey! Dig deep down inside and *really* mean it."

No, instead He was saying, "Allow Me to give your heart a transforming revelation of My love for that person!" Forgive *from*—or *starting*—in the heart.

In *His* heart, God sees us through eyes of love. He imagines us in completion. He sees us redemptively.

> *We must get God's viewpoint in our heart—of ourselves of course, but also of our offenders.*

Only then can we see what He sees when we look at ourselves and at others.

Several years ago, I was going through a time of inner healing while reading the book *Shadow Boxing* by Henry Malone.[2] I was allowing the Lord to reveal to me anyone against whom I still held judgments, and He brought to my mind someone that I thought I had forgiven already.

Often, when I am praying with someone and leading them through releasing forgiveness, they will say, "Oh, I've already done that. I have forgiven them before." I will say to them that since Holy Spirit brought it up, perhaps they should just go ahead and forgive again.

Sure enough, God will take them to a *deeper healing and forgiveness*. That is how this instance was for me. The actual offense had occurred many years prior, and I had forgiven them a great deal.

Holy Spirit revealed to me this time though, the full circle of His redemptive plan. I saw that God had allowed the offense (which was great), because He saw down through the years of my timeline that this exact divine moment would come. This was a powerful moment in which I would choose to pray that God Almighty would take what the enemy had meant for evil and turn it for good.

I saw the wounds, insecurities, and deep needs within that person, and my heart felt God's compassion for them. Suddenly, I was enabled to become a conduit of His blessing. I prayed for my enemy, and by a miracle of God's grace, I meant it. I prayed every wonderful thing that I could think of for God to do for them, and by a miracle of God's grace, I wanted Him to. I forgave, and it wasn't a loss. It was a tremendous gain for *both* of us. (Note: That does not mean that I should have that person in my life again, and the same is true for you. Forgiveness often means releasing that harmful person and loving them *from a distance*.)

Are you ready? Ready to finally be free from that festering wound and debilitating anger? Now is your moment. *You* don't have to change your heart. You don't have to "dig down deeper" and squeeze out a drop of forgiveness. No, Jesus will change your heart by giving you *His view* of your offender when you let go and surrender your pain to Him.

I have, like many of you, experienced great hurt at the hands of people, but I can honestly say that I am free from offense. As God ministered to me the things I have shared here with you, I have glimpsed an awe-inspiring thing. I can't explain it, but I'm thankful for it all—the good, the bad, and the ugly. I can see now how God *really does work all things together for good*,[3] but not just *my* good. I can see now how His redemption comes as I forgive and bless those who spitefully used me or hurt me. You can *see* that in your life as well and find the freedom it brings!

Summary

- Forgiveness is a choice to release someone from the harm they have caused you. It isn't weak or losing, but rather it is strength and healing.
- Forgiveness starts from the heart where we get a true revelation from God about the person who has wronged us. We see them as God sees them and are able to have compassion upon them.
- Unforgiveness is sin, and it is an access point for demonic powers to have entrance into our life.
- Unforgiveness is a prison of our own making.
- The *choice* to forgive is the key to our freedom.
- When we pray for and bless our enemies, God can do a redemptive work in their lives.

Faith Declaration

"Just like my Jesus, I am a forgiver! I forgive quickly and freely from my heart."

Activation

- Ask the Father who you need to forgive. Write down each person He brings to mind even if it doesn't make sense to you.

- Pray the sample prayer from the section below for each name that you wrote down.

- Don't forget to forgive yourself. Pray like this, "Lord, I forgive myself for…" The list may be long or short; don't stop until you are *done*.

Prayer

Father, I choose to forgive this person, and I release them from the harm they have caused me. I hand them to You, and I ask You to bless them and work in their life in a miraculous and wonderful way just like You do for me, over and over. I hand to You the anger and the pain that I have held. In exchange, I ask You to fill me with Your amazing love for this person. Lord, forgive me for any judgments I have put on this person. God, right now I hand to You the lenses of hatred, hurt, resentment, and unforgiveness that I have viewed this person through, and TODAY I ask You to give me YOUR view of them and Your heart towards them. Father, finally, please tell me the truth that You want me to know about them. Amen.

- Now, take the time to listen. God will give you a picture or revelation concerning your offender that will create compassion in you and enable you to truly forgive from the heart. *It is your healing balm.*

ACCESS POINT 4: JUDGMENTS AND INNER VOWS

*J*udgments are one of the five open doors through which the enemy can have *legal access* to our lives, our "land." When we judge, we reap judgment. In scripture, there are many examples of the law of sowing and reaping. Here are a few:

> "Jesus said, 'Forsake the habit of criticizing and judging others, and then you will not be criticized and judged in return. Don't look at others and pronounce them guilty, and you will not experience guilty accusations yourself. Forgive over and over and you will be forgiven over and over. Give generously and generous gifts will be given back to you, shaken down to make room for more. Abundant gifts will pour out upon you with such an overflowing measure that it will run over the top! Your measurement of generosity becomes the measurement of your return.'"

> — LUKE 6:37-38, TPT

"What happiness comes to you when you feel your spiritual poverty! For theirs is the realm of heaven's kingdom. "What delight comes to you when you wait upon the Lord! For you will find what you long for. "What blessing comes to you when gentleness lives in you! For you will inherit the earth. "How enriched you are when you crave righteousness! For you will be surrounded with fruitfulness. How satisfied you are when you demonstrate tender mercy! For tender mercy will be demonstrated to you. "What bliss you experience when your heart is pure! For then your eyes will open to see more and more of God. "How joyful you are when you make peace! For then you will be recognized as a true child of God. "How enriched you are when you bear the wounds of being persecuted for doing what is right! For that is when you experience the realm of heaven's kingdom."

— MATTHEW 5:3-10, TPT

"Ask, and the gift is yours. Seek, and you'll discover. Knock, and the door will be opened for you."

— MATTHEW 7:7, TPT

Most of these are positive, but one promise is actually a bit of a warning. It is also a key to a life of freedom: judge not, and ye shall not be judged. In the Message version it reads like this:

"Don't pick on people, jump on their failures, criticize their faults — unless, of course, you want the same treatment. That critical spirit has a way of boomeranging. It's easy to see a smudge on your neighbor's face and be oblivious to the ugly sneer on your own. Do you have the nerve to say, 'Let me wash your face for you,' when your own face is distorted by contempt? It's this whole traveling road-show mentality all over again, playing a holier-than-thou part instead of just living your part. Wipe that ugly sneer off your own face, and you might be fit to offer a washcloth to your neighbor."

— MATTHEW 7:1-5, MSG

The Apostle Paul exhorts us similarly:

"If you do not sit in judgment of others, you will avoid judgment yourself."

— 1 CORINTHIANS 11:31, TPT

Yikes! That one command alone would make our Christian message much more palatable to the world if only we lived it.

First of all, it must be noted that this scripture is probably one of the most misused verses in the Bible. I mean, haven't we all at some time or other heard an unbeliever hurl this scripture ("Judge not, lest you be judged!") as a cannonball of accusation? Many times Christians *are* condemning and finger-pointing, and this is so counterproductive.

Jesus was a friend of sinners, and He actually used His harshest words when speaking to religious hypocrites. He drew people (and *still* draws people) with cords of love and bands of mercy (Hosea 11:4). Indeed, His kindness is what leads us to repentance. His love, His wooing, His kisses, and *His embrace* changes us. In fact, God will hug us into holiness if we let Him! Grace *saves*, so why would we ever imagine that angry judgment could *transform*?

So, what is the real meaning to be understood from this verse? This verse is God teaching us:

"My child, you are not the judge of a person's heart."

I personally find this aspect of God's nature and character very comforting and safe, don't you? Think about it. He reserves the right to assess the hearts of all people. The One who *alone* has the power over our body, soul, and spirit is the only One allowed to judge us. He is so safe, and His word says that mercy triumphs over judgment. Evidently, He has written a loophole into His own law!

I may judge fruit. I may judge actions and sins. However, I may not drop the gavel on a fellow human, in my heart.

We all know that gossip is wrong. It is evil. Think of judgment as gossip in the heart. If I have sinned in this manner, I may or may not vocalize it, but deep inside my heart a judgment has been made about a person, and I have condemned them to a certain category or label. When we cast judgments against someone in our hearts, we have "pigeon-holed" them and filed them away.

Why do we feel justified in doing this? I believe it is a version of pride in one of its most devious forms, because, in order to judge someone and write them off, I must basically deem myself worthier. It is a holier-than-thou heart issue, and it is a *major trap*.

Judgments are one of the five open doors through which the enemy can have *legal access* to our lives, our land. When we judge, we reap judgment. It happens so subtly. This is something that I did habitually throughout my life without really realizing it until God's word brought light into this dark area.

Judgments don't always sound distinctly like judgments. Sometimes they're not direct. Sometimes they sound like this:

- "He is not a good leader."

- "They are simple-minded."

- "She wouldn't get it."

- "They got what they deserved."

- "He has is clueless."

- "They would be lost without me."

- "They don't appreciate me."

- "She thinks she is all that."

- "He is never going to amount to anything."

- "She is an irresponsible person."

- "She is a know-it-all."

- "He isn't worth my time."

Again, the *actions* of the people around us may back up these assumptions, however, we are not appointed as the judge of them! We *may not* put them in the box of our prideful labeling. When we view those in our lives through the lenses of judgment and condemnation and pride, we *cannot* at the same time see them as God does.

We can't judge someone's heart and love them at the same time.

We simply can't. It's one way or the other. Either we are on the Lord's side, or we are on the side of the accuser. It's scary, but it's true.

Judgment is a Pride Issue

"Then in the middle of his teaching, the religious scholars and the Pharisees broke through the crowd and brought a woman who had been caught in the act of committing adultery and made her stand in the middle of everyone. Then they said to Jesus, 'Teacher, we caught this woman in the very act of adultery. Doesn't Moses' law command us to stone to death a woman like this? Tell us, what do you say we should do with her?' They were only testing Jesus because they hoped to trap him with his own words and accuse him of breaking the laws of Moses. But Jesus didn't answer them. Instead he simply bent down and wrote in the dust with his finger. Angry, they kept insisting that he answer their question, so Jesus stood up and looked at them and said, 'Let's have the man who has never had a sinful desire throw the first stone at her.' And then he bent over again and wrote some more words in the dust. Upon hearing that, her accusers slowly left the crowd one at a time, beginning with the oldest to the youngest, with a convicted conscience. Until finally, Jesus was left alone with the woman still standing there in front of him. So he stood back up and said to her, 'Dear woman, where are your accusers? Is there no one here to condemn you?' Looking around, she replied, 'I see no one, Lord.' Jesus said, 'Then I certainly don't condemn you either. Go, and from now on, be free from a life of sin.' Then Jesus said, 'I am light to the world and those who embrace me will experience life-giving light, and they will never walk in darkness.'"

— JOHN 8:3-12, TPT

What a beautiful story. What a revealing demonstration of God's heart for the broken and the sinful. The backdrop to this event was the feast of tabernacles. The day before Jesus had stood and made a bold proclamation.

"All you thirsty ones, come to me! Come to me and drink! Believe in me so that rivers of living water will burst out from within you, flowing from your innermost being, just like the Scripture says!"

— JOHN 7:37-38, TPT

During this feast, the men customarily proclaimed this prophetic passage from Jeremiah:

"Hope of Isra'el, ADONAI! All who abandon you will be ashamed, those who leave you will be inscribed in the dust, because they have abandoned ADONAI, the source of living water."

— JEREMIAH 17:13, CJB

All the men in this prideful and rigidly self-righteous crowd of accusers knew exactly what reference Jesus was making when He knelt and inscribed in the dust. He was illustrating who the true adulterers were—the spiritual adulterers—who had abandoned the source of living water, Jesus. What conviction must have come over their hearts in that moment as each one knew that scripture and also knew the law which required that both the woman *and the adulterous man* (plus a witness) were to be presented before the priest. Everything was wrong with what they were attempting that day, and the greatest error was their own wayward hearts. They had abandoned Adonai, and Jesus exposed their religious pride.

A Log and A Speck

"Why do you look at the speck that is in your brother's eye, but do not notice the log that is in your own eye? Or how can you say to your brother, 'Let me take the speck out of your eye,' and behold, the log is in your own eye? You hypocrite, first take the log out of your own eye, and then you will see clearly to take the speck out of your brother's eye."

— MATTHEW 7:3-5, NASB

This is a very familiar passage, and we can become *so* familiar with it that we could easily miss some important truths. Let's take a fresh look. First of all, notice that Jesus warns us not to focus on specks. Selah. Aren't we so prone to do that? It seems that we draw a twisted comfort by finding and pointing out the faults of others. Somehow, we tend to feel better about our ourselves when we can shine the light on the shortcomings of others. How sad and shallow. Plus, Jesus implies that it is folly—foolishness! For how very impaired our own vision is when it is crowded and clouded by sin and pride.

Furthermore, Jesus poses a question, "How can you help someone else when you have the same problem yourself?" What hypocrisy!

Finally, let's consider the most important question here. Can you be a very compassionate "surgeon" to another person if you have never gone under the knife yourself? Put yourself in the place of the pitiful person walking around with an enormous log protruding from their eye. We must put ourselves in that place, because truthfully we *are* in that place. None of us is perfect.

Humility is key to helping others. Jesus wants us to know that, but I believe He also wants us to know that once we do deal with our log, that the difficult, painful, humbling (you can't do it alone), and long process *changes us.* After such a process, we are not only healthier and happier, but we are equipped with deep compassion to carefully, gently, and patiently help others with their own specks. We know how it hurts. We know how a kind touch and comforting word during the process is so very precious. Jesus wants loving, speck surgeons! And I am so thankful for that, aren't you? I would much rather be operated on by a scalpel than an ax. Spiritually, I have had both, and the ax may get the job done but just creates more specks for the future as I will need healing from the clumsy spiritual surgery that ended up wounding my soul.

There Is Only One Lawgiver and Judge

"Be willing to be made low before the Lord and he will exalt you! Dear friends, as part of God's family, never speak against another family member, for when you slander a brother or sister you violate God's law of love. And your duty is not to make yourself a judge of the law of love by saying that it doesn't apply to you, but your duty is to obey it! There is only one true Lawgiver and Judge, the One who has the power to save and destroy—so who do you think you are to judge your neighbor?"

—JAMES 4:10-12, TPT

"Who do you think you are to sit in judgment of someone else's household servant? His own master is the one to evaluate whether he succeeds or fails. And God's servants will succeed, for God's power supports them and enables them to stand."

— ROMANS 14:4, TPT

Wow. We really see God's amazing heart here for His servants. *He is able to make His servants stand.* I want to be on the Lord's side! I want to be full of His heart, standing with Him as He helps, strengthens, and cheers people on to be the *best* He intends for them to be, always remembering that no matter how people may look, how they may fall or fail (don't we all), *their story is still being read from heaven!* It ain't over.

We are all on the journey to transformation.

Maybe I am further along than someone else, or maybe they are miles ahead of me, but we are all on time. Why? Because God is able to make us stand. He is and always will be working in our lives according to His master plan, His blueprint, the *imago*.

This brings to mind the famous story of Michelangelo and his sculpture of David. It is said that he saw David in a chunk of marble and then chipped away the surplus. In a similar way, God sees each of us as who we really are and deals with us through redemption to release that image. He didn't come and die for us to condemn us, but to save us. That is His heart.

I don't know about you, but this teaching puts the holy fear of the Lord in my heart. I *need* mercy! I don't want judgment on my own life, not from other people and not from God. I want to shut that door to the enemy and put up a no trespassing sign!

How do we do that? Well, judgment (placing judgment on others) is a sin, and the good news is that *all* sin has already been dealt with at the cross. We only need to confess it and repent of it. We can also speak blessings on those we have judged! What better way to take the spoils of war, making sure that what the enemy meant for evil gets used for good.

We are meant to be a conduit of God's love. God's love changes lives. The enemy works overtime to do whatever He can to stop up the flow of the love. *You can be sure that in whatever area you are holding onto judgment, you are withholding love.* Let it go so that you can bring Heaven into the situation.

When we are able to make the transition from victim to forgiver, we step into a *very powerful position.* When we choose to partner with God over a person's life, we release ourselves from the trap of bitterness and a victim mentality by becoming one who blesses and not one who judges.

Inner Vows

What is an inner vow? If you are like me, you have heard very little, or possibly no teaching, on this subject. Similar to judgments, inner vows also take place deep inside our hearts. They are seemingly little decisions that we make, with a unique twist. Inner vows are our human, soulish attempt to control something.

These insidious decisions are on the level of witchcraft, because we are basically attempting to use soul power to make something happen or to keep something from happening.

In short, an inner vow is a solemn promise you make to yourself, usually in a moment of pain, in an effort to soothe your wounded soul. Inner vows have the potential to create a wall between you and God when they contradict the truth of who you are in Christ.

Here are a few examples:

- A girl growing up with an abusive father may make a vow, "I will never trust a man."

- Growing up with a drug addicted sibling may tempt a child to vow, "I will never do drugs."

- Growing up in poverty may make a child vow, "I will never be poor when I grow up."

- If a child grew up with an alcoholic father, they may make this *judgment*, "My dad was a loser." But, at the same time, they may make this *vow*, "I will never get married." Later, the *fruit* may be that she becomes homosexual.

As these examples show, most inner vows are made by us when we are young. An inner vow is like a hard place in our heart where fear has taught us that we must maintain a strangle-hold on control in order to protect ourselves.

Obviously, from these bitter root vows and judgments grow much sinful fruit. The manifestations may be obvious, but they can be quite subtle as well. Who would think that a vow to never be a drunk could result in a life bound by addiction? Who would think that a vow to never be like one's parent could result in a cycle of abuse being perpetuated in the next generation? But it so often does.

Soul Power Versus God's Power

The reason is very simple, and thankfully so is the cure. When we willfully say, "I will never," we are kicking God out of that authority place in our heart and, in essence, giving the enemy access to it. *An inner vow is an open door for the enemy.*

As soon as a person makes such a vow, the enemy seizes his opportunity. He gladly takes over that little piece of real estate in our lives and starts building his stronghold. A stronghold is a battle term. It is a base of military action. The enemy works very hard to establish a base of operation *within our soul.* I'm not talking about demon possession, but I am talking about torment, struggle, weakness, and often defeat. Why defeat? Because if we have enemies in our land, winning is not likely! It is high time we serve these spirits an eviction notice.

Instead of inner vows, *speak God's word* over your life! Proclaim His promises. Use your faith in God, not your soul power.

> "Again, you have heard that the ancients were told, 'YOU SHALL NOT MAKE FALSE VOWS, BUT SHALL FULFILL YOUR VOWS TO THE LORD.' But I say to you, make no oath at all, either by heaven, for it is the throne of God, or by the earth, for it is the footstool of His feet, or by Jerusalem, for it is THE CITY OF THE GREAT KING. Nor shall you make an oath by your head, for you cannot make one hair white or black. But let your statement be, 'Yes, yes' or 'No, no'; anything beyond these is of evil."
>
> — MATTHEW 5:33-37, NASB

> "But above all, my brethren, do not swear, either by heaven or by earth or with any other oath. But let your 'Yes' be 'Yes,' and your 'No,' 'No', lest you fall into judgment."
>
> —JAMES 5:12

"So then, surrender to God. Stand up to the devil and resist him and he will turn and run away from you. Move your heart closer and closer to God, and he will come even closer to you. But make sure you cleanse your life, you sinners, and keep your heart pure and stop doubting."

—JAMES 4:7-8, TPT

Summary

- The enemy gains access to your life when you make judgments against another person and when you make inner vows.
- Judging a human heart is only God's job, never ours.
- When I walk in judgment, I open the door for others and God to judge me.
- I cannot judge and love at the same time.
- Inner vows may feel like protection, but it is a counterfeit of the true protection of God.
- Scriptures for deeper study: Luke 6:37-38 TPT, 1 Corinthians 11:31 TPT, Ephesians 4:15 TPT, James 4:10-12 TPT, Romans 14:4 TPT, Matthew 5:33-37, and James 5:12.

Prayer

Father, thank You for revealing these truths to my life. Now I know! Forgive me for being a judge. Forgive me also for rebelliously using my own soul power to get my way in life and to self-protect. I repent, and I ask You to keep me from these pitfalls in the future. Please help me to guard my heart from these specific sins. Help me to have a clean heart towards my fellow man so that You can use me to bring Your love to them. In Jesus' name, I pray. Amen.

Faith Declaration

"I am a lover not a judger."

Activation

- Ask God to show you any judgments that you hold in your heart. As He shows you each one, repent and release the person. Pray a blessing upon them.

- Ask God to show you any inner vows that you have said in your heart or with your mouth. Repent of and renounce those vows. Ask God to come into those areas and do His will.

- Inner vows erect walls around your heart. Once you have repented of the vows, it's time to ask God to tear down the walls. These walls keep you from intimacy with God and with people.

- *Pray this: "Father, show me my wall."*
- *You may see, feel, or sense a barrier of some kind. Identify your "wall."*
- *Say, "Father, I ask you to tear down these walls of self-protection."*
- *Look and sense what changed in your wall. Is it unchanged, gone, partially gone?*
- *If it is gone, cross over to the other side. If it is still intact, ask God to show you who you need to forgive and let Him lead you through that repentance and forgiveness. Then again pray the wall down and walk through to the other side letting the Lord reveal to you what the wall was keeping you from.*
- *Finally, ask the Lord to help you not to rebuild that defense system and to help you form the healthy habit of trusting in His protection and strength.*

ACCESS POINT 5: CURSES

*U*nfortunately, this can be a controversial topic in the body of Christ. I'm not going to take the time to argue the point that curses can operate in the life of a believer. I truly believe, if we are honest with ourselves, we must admit curses are an issue that can't be ignored. We really need to accept that fact and go on to the real question. The real question is, why are curses *allowed* to operate in a person's life?

There is a very interesting verse in Proverbs that helps bring light on this subject.

"An undeserved curse will be powerless to harm you. It may flutter over you like a bird, but it will find no place to land."

— Proverbs 26:2, TPT

"Like the sparrow in her wandering, like the swallow in her flying, So the curse without cause does not come and alight [on the undeserving]."

— Proverbs 26:2, AMP

The Cause

We see clearly here that we have nothing to fear from curses, and they cannot light or land (picture a nesting bird) on us at all *unless there is a cause*. So essentially, if a curse is in operation, there must be a reason. *There must be a cause.*

This leads to the obvious question: What are the causes? Scripture teaches, or actually warns, of sins that result in curses. Here is a list of some of the primary causes.

Causes of Curses

1. Disrespect and disobedience to parents

2. Acknowledging or worshipping false gods

3. Involvement with the occult

4. Mistreating the weak and defenseless

5. All forbidden, aberrant, or unlawful sexual relationships

6. Anti-Semitism

7. Dependence on human strength, wisdom or goodness

8. Words spoken by those in authority

9. Stealing and lying

10. Words spoken against ourselves

11. Oaths or covenants taken for admission into secret societies and ungodly organizations

12. Curses pronounced by witches, occultists or witchdoctors

13. Carnal talk directed at others

14. Witchcraft prayer (manipulative)

(Credit to *Shadow Boxing* by Henry Malone.[1])

Generational Curses

In addition to these sins that an individual may commit which give cause to a curse, there is also the issue of generational curses.

Believe it or not, this topic excites me, and I hope that after learning more about it, you get a little excited, too! The reason I get excited is because when we begin to talk about *generational* topics, we can begin to see the *big picture*. I guarantee you with full assurance that the demonic realm actively works to keep these truths hidden from believers. Why? Because these demonic forces do not want to leave their "home."

> "When a demon is cast out of a person, it roams around a dry region, looking for a place to rest, but never finds it. Then it says, 'I'll return to the house I moved out of,' and so it goes back, only to find that the house is vacant, warm, and ready for it to move back in. So it goes looking for seven other demons more evil than itself, and they all enter together to live there. Then the person's condition becomes much worse than it was in the beginning. This describes what will also happen to the people of this evil generation."
>
> — MATTHEW 12:43-45, TPT

You see, this issue of freedom is much bigger than you. By that, I don't mean that your enemy is bigger, no way! I mean the repercussions of your freedom are far-reaching.

The potential outcome of your freedom is literally exponential!

Let me paint the picture. In this lesson that Jesus teaches about the house, we see that the evil spirit was cast out. Why isn't that the end of the story? I mean, shouldn't that be the end of the story? No, there are some important steps that need to be taken *by the believer* to maintain their freedom and keep their house free. Let's look again:

> "Now when the unclean spirit goes out of a man, it passes through waterless places seeking rest, and does not find it. Then it says, 'I will return to my house from which I came'; and when it comes, it finds it unoccupied, swept, and put in order. Then it goes and takes along with it seven other spirits more wicked than itself, and they go in and live there; and the last state of that man becomes worse than the first. That is the way it will also be with this evil generation."
>
> — MATTHEW 12:43-45, NASB

Clean and Filled

Why was the evil spirit able to come back? Jesus said it is because the home was vacant. What does this mean for you and I on a very practical level? We are responsible to fill our home (our heart and life) with the presence, words, and service of God. Essentially, *we must crowd out the devil!* It is such a simple concept but widely overlooked. I promise you, if you are not willing to *choose* to crowd out the influences of the enemy in your life, Satan will *take the opportunity* to crowd out God. Let me say it plainly, the devil is cast out *and* crowded out. It is our responsibility to give him *no opportunity in our life.*

> "Don't give the slanderous accuser, the Devil, an opportunity to manipulate you!"
>
> — EPHESIANS 4:27, TPT

Prayerfully examine your spiritual home (your heart and life). Once you have been swept clean, be sure you are furnishing your life in such a way that even seven more wicked spirits would not be able to penetrate the glory of God surrounding you! It is entirely possible. In fact, it is a covenant blessing to the obedient.

> "The LORD shall cause your enemies who rise up against you to be defeated before you; they will come out against you one way and will flee before you seven ways."
>
> — DEUTERONOMY 28:7, NASB

Rest assured that when you are living by His life, walking in purity, and following in the footsteps of Jesus, devils are absolutely fleeing in your wake, seven different ways!

> "So then, surrender to God. Stand up to the devil and resist him and he will turn and run away from you."
>
> —JAMES 4:7, TPT

A Bigger Picture

This is all good information (understatement), but you may be thinking, "What does it have to do with generational curses?"

When I look at the passage about the seven devils, I also see an additional application to my life other than just my own personal freedom. *I also see my "house" as my bloodline.* Enforcing and maintaining my own personal freedom is amazing, but again, there is a *much bigger picture.*

Think of the story of David in scripture. When he took down Goliath, it meant so much for him personally, didn't it? It opened his life up to a totally new realm of favor, promotion, influence, and blessings. He literally stepped out of one reality into another! Everything changed for him. This is what gaining personal freedom is like!

> "So if the Son sets you free from sin, then become a true son and be unquestionably free!"
>
> —JOHN 8:36, TPT

I love that! Unquestionably free sounds so good! Additionally, because of David's victory on that battlefield, his lineage was also forever radically changed. The entire line of David *became* royalty. In fact, Jesus himself was called the Son of David. God's promise to David was that he would always have a descendant on the throne, and he will through Jesus Christ.

David's victory was completely based on his intimate relationship with God. It is the same for us. As we gain victory over our enemies, walking onto the battlefield in the armor of God and the power of Christ's shed blood, as we take off the head of OUR giants, *we ensure that our descendants won't have to.*

My victories are the spiritual inheritances laid up for my children. Every time I defeat a stronghold in my own life, it *is* bigger than me because it is for my children and my children's children to a *thousand* generations! Woohoo! Receive that amazing truth.

> "Be mindful of His covenant forever, The promise which He commanded and established to a thousand generations..."
>
> — 1 CHRONICLES 16:15, AMP

> "You shall not worship them or serve them [false gods]; for I, the LORD your God, am a jealous God, visiting the iniquity of the fathers on the children, and on the third and the fourth generations of those who hate Me, but showing lovingkindness to thousands, to those who love Me and keep My commandments."
>
> — DEUTERONOMY 5:9-10, NASB

Obviously our children will still have battles to fight, and they will deal with sin. But they should not have to deal with a generational curse left in operation in our bloodline because we as parents were lazy or passive. It should be our desire that they take *new territory!* Not for them to have to fight to regain what we lost or failed to possess.

Get Out Of My House, My Heart, and My Home!

I can evict the devil from my house (bloodline), from my heart, and from my home, from my personal life and from my physical dwelling. This. Is. Exciting. You and I may have had to deal with extreme fear, but our children don't have to. We may have had to break cycles of abuse, but our children don't have to. We may have to spiritually take off the head of the giant of chronic health problems, but our children don't have to!

Can't you just hear the knocking knees of your adversary? He does not want to leave his home. He does not want to wander out in dry places. He may have had a recliner and Netflix set up in your bloodline, living in ease for many generations, but it is your blood bought right and privilege to kick him out and put up the no trespassing sign. Cast him out, and crowd him out. Resist the devil, and he will flee! Do it for you *and* for your future generations.

> "…and they said, 'Believe on the Lord Jesus Christ, and thou shalt be saved [saved, healed, and delivered]--thou and thy house."
>
> — Acts 16:31, AMP

> "This day I call the heavens and the earth as witnesses against you that I have set before you life and death, blessings and curses. Now choose life, so that you and your descendants may live, by loving and obeying God, and holding fast to him."
>
> — Deuteronomy 30:19-20, NASB

Please don't feel overwhelmed or afraid when it comes to this topic! Curses are the result of sin, and therefore have been taken care of *already* at the cross. In the same way that your sins were atoned for, curses have been broken as well.

> "Yet, Christ paid the full price to set us free from the curse of the law. He absorbed it completely as he became a curse in our place. For it is written: 'Everyone who is hung upon a tree is doubly cursed.' Jesus, our Messiah, was cursed in our place and in so doing, dissolved the curse from our lives, so that all the blessings of Abraham can be poured out upon even non-Jewish believers. And now God gives us the promise of the wonderful Holy Spirit who lives within us when we believe in him."

> — GALATIANS 3:13-14, TPT

However, you and I know that forgiveness for sins must still be appropriated. Jesus became my sin on the cross, and He bore my curses, but I still must confess my sin and ask for forgiveness. In the same way, I also must confess and repent of my sins and the sins of my ancestors that have resulted in curses having a *cause to operate* in my life. I must do my part.

My Part

> "The descendants of Israel (Jacob) separated themselves from all foreigners, and stood and confessed their sins and the wrongdoings of their fathers."

> — NEHEMIAH 9:2, AMP

(If you don't know where to start, there is a sample prayer provided at the end of the chapter, and it would be a good place to begin!)

All curses, like all sin, are broken at the cross. Hallelujah! Your part of confession and repentance through faith in Christ's shed blood removes the cause and revokes the power of any curse, for yourself and all your future generations. That's *real* power!

Check out this powerful, real-life example of generational legacy:

Jonathan Edwards, was a Puritan Preacher in the 1700s. He was one of the most respected preachers in his day. He attended Yale at the age of thirteen and later went on to become the president of Princeton college. He married his wife Sarah in 1727 and they were blessed with eleven children. Every night when Mr. Edwards was home, he would spend an hour conversing with his family and then praying a blessing over each child. Jonathan and his wife Sarah passed on a great, godly legacy to their eleven children.

An American educator, A.E. Winship decided to trace the descendants of Jonathan Edwards almost 150 years after his death. His findings are remarkable, especially when compared to another man from the same time period known as Max Jukes.

Jonathan Edwards' legacy includes one U.S. vice president, one dean of a law school, one dean of a medical school, three U.S. senators, three governors, three mayors, thirteen college presidents, thirty judges, sixty doctors, sixty-five professors, seventy-five military officers, eighty public office holders, one-hundred lawyers, 200 clergymen, and 285 college graduates.

How may this be explained? Edwards was a godly man, but he was also hard working, intelligent and moral. Furthermore, Winship states, "Much of the capacity and talent, intensity and character of the more than 1,400 of Edwards' family is due to Mrs. Edwards."

Max Jukes's legacy came to people's attention when the family trees of 42 different men in the New York prison system were traced back to him. He lived in New York at about the same period as Edwards. The Jukes family originally was studied by sociologist Richard L. Dugdale in 1877.

Jukes's descendants includes seven murderers, sixty thieves, 190 prostitutes, 150 other convicts, 310 paupers, and 440 who were physically wrecked by addiction to alcohol. Of the 1,200 descendants that were studied, 300 died prematurely.[2]

Summary

- Curses cannot be in operation in my life unless there is a cause.
- Often, the cause is my disobedience or the disobedience of my ancestors.
- Confession, repentance, and receiving God's forgiveness is the remedy for sin.
- Once my "house" is cleansed of sin, I am responsible to fill it with the things of God.
- If I don't actively fill my life and crowd out the enemy, he will encroach and attempt to crowd out God.
- When I choose blessing over curses, I am choosing it for my whole house and for my future generations.
- Scriptures for further study: Proverbs 26:2, Matthew 12:43-45, James 4:7, Deuteronomy 30:19-20a, Galatians 3:13-14, Nehemiah 9:2

Faith Declaration

"I choose life for me and my house forever. I am blessed!"

Activation

- Ask the Lord to bring to mind any word curses that have been spoken over you by yourself or anyone else (especially those in authority over your life like parents, teachers, pastors, etc.).

- Forgive each person (including yourself), and release them from any harm they brought to your life.

- Declare those false labels are removed from your life by the name and the blood of Jesus.

- Speak the opposite. In other words replace the lying label with truth. For example, "I am not unwanted; I was planned and chosen by God."

- Make sure you write down those declarations! Say them out loud daily for a month or longer. By doing this, you are actually rewriting your thought patterns and changing your brain!

A JOB TRIAL

"We honor them as our heroes because they remained faithful even while enduring great sufferings. And you have heard of all that Job went through and we can now see that the Lord ultimately treated him with wonderful kindness, revealing how tenderhearted he really is!"

—JAMES 5:11, TPT

I do want to make mention of a type of trial that is also sometimes necessary warfare. It is actually in a category all of its own, and it is what I refer to as a Job trial.

A Job trial just can't be filed away neatly in our nice Christian filing system because it doesn't make sense. It won't make sense to those around you (usually), and often it won't even make sense to you.

It is difficult beyond words. It will take you to a place where you would never choose to go on your own. Like Daniel's lion's den, Shadrach, Meshach, and Abednego's fiery furnace, Paul's lonely imprisonments, Jesus' wilderness temptation and garden of Gethsemane--God leads you there for His purpose.

Because Job trials don't make sense, it can result in a time of great confusion and questioning. Just like with Job, most (if not all) your friends will try to counsel you but *not out of the heart of the Lord*. They may see the many things you should or shouldn't do and will unfortunately be quick to find fault, having all the right words but not the right spirit, and it will hurt.

An insightful part of Job's trial was his interactions with his three friends: Eliphaz, Bildad, and Zohar. These well-meaning but misinformed men are pictures of the attacks we experience in our trial.

The meaning of the name Eliphaz is "the endeavor of God."[1] He represents the people who come to get the speck out of our eye, but their work on us is clumsy and painful because they have an enormous obstacle (a log) in the way. They desire to be your junior Holy Spirit and do "the endeavor of God" in your life, but it's like having surgery performed with a butcher knife--harsh, callous, overbearing, and painful! The Eliphaz types operate in a religious, holier-than-thou spirit and make you feel hopeless.

The name Bildad means "old friendship."[2] He represents those who want to tie you to your past. The accusing voices asking, "Who do you think you are?" come from the Bildad types in our life. Their intimidation eats away at our identity, faith, and confidence in God's heart for us.

The name Zophar means "doubtful" and also "chirping, rising early."[3] This represents the grating on our hearts and minds from the constant chatter of doubt and what-ifs. We must stay in a place of worship and grateful love in order to not be weighted down, disheartened, or discouraged by these voices. Also, we must always remember that we don't wrestle with flesh and blood.[4] It is Satan who is behind these tactics.

As it was for Job, this trial will likely be a time of great accusation from the enemy. He will bombard you with all your faults and failures attempting to cause you to doubt God's commitment to your wellbeing. You may fear for your life, or at your lowest point you may even wish for death. *The enemy would love nothing more than to kill the dreams you have for your future.*

There was another so-called friend who also came on the scene in Job's low point. His name was Elihu, whose name means "my god is he."[5] Some believe Elihu represents Holy Spirit, but I disagree. In my opinion, Elihu represents the most insidious voice of all, that of an angel of light. This voice sounds *so right* that we mistake it for the voice of God.

Listen to Elihu's words, "For truly my words are not false; one who is perfect in knowledge is with you" (Job 36:4, NIV). This voice is the one we hear in our deepest, darkest moments and tells us the lies that have the potential to completely knock us off course. Again, it's the most insidious voice of all because we can confuse it with Holy Spirit. This voice whispers, "Has God truly said?"[6] and "If you are the Son of God…"[7]

This voice comes in the midst of the trial and makes us really begin to entertain the idea that it is all our fault after all, or that we deserve what happened. This voice tries to tell us God is against us. When we fall to this lying voice, we can lose all hope and enter into despair.

One important thing to know is that only "Jobs" are chosen for a Job trial. Being allowed by God to endure such a fiery furnace, I truly believe, is a precious commendation from God. Let's take a look at this heavenly conversation.

> "Then the Lord said to Satan, 'Have you considered my servant Job? There is no one on earth like him; he is blameless and upright, a man who fears God and shuns evil.' 'Does Job fear God for nothing?' Satan replied. 'Have you not put a hedge around him and his household and everything he has? You have blessed the work of his hands, so that his flocks and herds are spread throughout the land. But now stretch out your hand and strike everything he has, and he will surely curse you to your face.' The Lord said to Satan, 'Very well, then, everything he has is in your

power, but on the man himself do not lay a finger.' Then Satan
went out from the presence of the Lord."

—Job 1:8-12, NIV

I see a Father in this passage. God intimately knew His servant Job.
He knew Job's heart, and so He allowed the testing. However, this
was not just an arbitrary decision, even though on the surface it may
appear so. God would never do that. He doesn't waste our pain.

> "May the thought of this [your salvation] cause you to jump for
> joy, even though lately you've had to put up with the grief of
> many trials. But these only reveal the sterling core of your faith,
> which is far more valuable than gold that perishes, for even gold is
> refined by fire. Your authentic faith will result in even more praise,
> glory, and honor when Jesus the Anointed One is revealed."
>
> — 1 Peter 1:6-7, TPT

There is purpose in the pain. Never doubt it. The fire of affliction
purifies, perfects, and proves our faith. After the trial, we are
changed. A quality is brought forth. A refinement is made possible.
But the greatest blessing of all is the deep, deep intimacy that is
cultivated. From that intimacy, a *fruitfulness* previously unattained
begins to spring forth.

Lessons From the Fire

I went through a trial like this a few years back. I thought I had
been through trials before, but this was beyond anything I'd ever
experienced. It lasted forty days, and those days for me were mostly
spent praying or weeping. I felt so many things, but one overriding
impression I experienced was the sense that I was walking on water,
walking by faith like never before. Let me tell you, it was not as
much fun and excitement as I had previously imagined when

reading Peter's water-walking story in the Bible! There were times when I was terrified.

I had to be so vigilant to keep my eyes on Jesus. If I looked at circumstances or at the winds and waves, I would sink and drown in my emotions. I can honestly say that I grew some major faith muscles during that time. I grew. I also had precious, precious encounters with my Jesus during that time that I wouldn't trade for anything.

> "I am convinced that any suffering we endure is less than nothing compared to the magnitude of glory that is about to be unveiled within us."
>
> — ROMANS 8:18, TPT

When I look into the face of Jesus one day, I guarantee you I will not be showing Him my battles wounds or telling Him any sad story. *It will all be so worth it.* No pain will be measured and no scar will be treasured on that day.

During that difficult time, I had an interesting conversation with Jesus. I was thinking about Job and all he went through. Then I thought about the fact that when Job's trial was over, he received double for his trouble.

If you read his story, you see that in the end everything that he lost (his children, his cattle, his reputation, and more) was restored to him fully, and then doubled! What an encouragement to our hearts.

Double For Our Trouble

I meditated on that. I talked to the Lord about how I wondered just how that was for Job. I told the Lord that if I were Job, I might rather have not had to get double for *any* trouble, you know? I pondered whether or not Job would have been better off if he had never gone through the trouble in the first place. I was just being real with God, because I know He is not afraid to be questioned.

A scripture then came to my mind from Holy Spirit about when Jesus was saying to His disciples that a woman forgets the pain of childbirth because of the joy that comes with the birth of a baby. Now, I've given birth to four children. I know a little about the pain of childbirth. I actually said to Jesus, "Are you sure about that?" I just couldn't imagine ever being able to forget the pain I was currently suffering.

I said to Jesus that I knew He had experienced humanity, but He hadn't ever given birth! I think I made Him laugh. I know I laughed, and I really needed to laugh right then!

We didn't ever really finish that conversation. I was just kind of hashing things out with the Lord and trying to get perspective. A few days later, I was receiving prayer and the woman ministering to me said that God had given her a very specific verse for me. She said that she argued a little with the Lord about it because it didn't seem like a very sweet and encouraging word, but the Lord assured her that she was indeed meant to give me the word. This is the verse she gave me:

> "Just like a woman giving birth experiences intense labor pains in delivering her baby, yet after the child is born she quickly forgets what she went through because of the overwhelming joy of knowing that a new baby has been born into the world. So will you also pass through a time of intense sorrow when I am taken from you, but you will see me again! And then your hearts will burst with joy, with no one being able to take it from you!"
>
> —JOHN 16:21-22, TPT

There is no one like our God! There is none sweeter than our Jesus. He is so kind, so near to the broken-hearted, so in touch with our needs. He is the best friend, ever. He was having a bit of fun with me that day! I will never forget it. It is a treasured memory, not a treasured scar.

About two months later, I thought back on that "Job trial." I thought, "Wow, Lord, it has already been two months since You broke through for me and did such miraculous things."

Then, I actually tried to remember how stressed, distressed, and terrible I had felt during the trial, and...I couldn't! Immediately, I remembered Jesus's promise to me that I wouldn't remember the pain, and I rejoiced! No one can take away that joy. It's mine. He gave it to me.

If you find yourself right now in such a fiery trial, I want to send love and strength and encouragement to your heart right now in the mighty name of Jesus. You are not alone. God is with you in the fire. He has got you. He knows you just like He knew Job. He knows that you are not going to walk away from Him or withdraw your affection from Him. He is so very proud of you! You are coming out of this fire like gold, and you are going to have the joy of the Lord. This fire is accomplishing something great. You need only to believe! You *will* receive double for all your trouble, but even more than that. Let's take a look at the end of the story to see what Job's *best* reward was.

> "I have heard of thee by the hearing of the ear: but now mine eye seeth thee."
>
> —Job 42:5, KJV

He had heard of God...but, after the trial of his life, He saw God. "Mine eye seeth thee," Job said. I believe that *seeing* God is an intimate encounter with Him. In Hebrew there is no word for "presence" but only the word that means "face." This is a beautiful picture of what it means to be in the presence of God. What a payback for your trouble! Intimate knowledge and face to face moments with Him, which are completely priceless. Yes Lord, I want that. Don't you? Look at the full response from Job after he got a clue.

"Job answered GOD: 'I'm convinced: You can do anything and everything. Nothing and no one can upset your plans. You asked, 'Who is this muddying the water, ignorantly confusing the issue, second-guessing my purposes?' I admit it. I was the one. I babbled on about things far beyond me, made small talk about wonders way over my head. You told me, 'Listen, and let me do the talking. Let me ask the questions. You give the answers.' I admit I once lived by rumors of you; now I have it all firsthand—from my own eyes and ears! I'm sorry—forgive me. I'll never do that again, I promise! I'll never again live on crusts of hearsay, crumbs of rumor."

—JOB 42:1-6, MSG

Aren't you glad you don't have to live on the "crusts of hearsay" and "crumbs of rumors" about God? He wants to and will make Himself known to His lovers. He is worth whatever trial takes us into that knowledge.

Since that conversation with Jesus where I jokingly told Him that He hadn't given birth, I have learned just how mistaken I was! *Jesus gave birth to the church.* His labor was His experience from Gethsemane (which means "oil press" and connotes a tremendous pressure), to the moment His cried out from the cross, "It is finished, My Bride!"[8]

The second Adam's side was pierced and water and blood poured forth symbolizing His beloved being brought forth—born—from His side like Eve came from the side of the first Adam.

"Beloved friends, if life gets extremely difficult, with many tests, don't be bewildered as though something strange were overwhelming you. Instead, continue to rejoice, for you, in a measure, have shared in the sufferings of the Anointed One so that you can share in the revelation of his glory and celebrate with even greater gladness!"

— 1 PETER 4:12-13, TPT

Oh yes, He understands when we suffer. He understands the results (birthing something new and wonderful) as well as the pain. And, He cares, which we will discuss in the next chapter.

Summary

- Not all warfare will fit nicely into our doctrinal boxes.
- Job trials are confusing, lonely, and extreme.
- God is *never* playing games with your pain. There is always purpose in your pain.
- If you find yourself in a Job trial, it is not because you did something wrong. Don't listen to accusations from people or the enemy...or yourself.
- Endure patiently. The trial will end, you will be rewarded, and no one will be able to take away your joy!
- Scripture verses for deeper study: Job, 1Peter 1:6-7, Romans 8:18, John 16:21-22, James 5:11, 1 Corinthians 10:13, and 1Peter 4:12-14

Prayer

Father, I praise You, and I thank You that You are King of my life. You hold all my times and seasons in Your very capable and loving hands. I don't go through anything without Your oversight, protection, and purpose. I trust You to always have my best at heart. You love me, and You will never allow me to be tested beyond what I am able to endure. I may feel like I can't take any more, but You know me better, and You always know best. I love You, Lord. Even if You never do another miracle for me, I will still love You. It's not what You do, but it's who You are that makes me love You. I know that I am the apple of Your eye, and I want You to know that You are also the apple of my eye. Today, right now, You are the center of my focus. It's all about You, Lord, and it always will be. I'm so in love with You, and I'm so grateful to be able to say that. You deserve all my love and worship forever. Amen.

Faith Declaration

"Even when I can't understand You, I can trust Your faithful love for me. You are trustworthy!"

Activation

- Picture yourself on that storm tossed sea, walking toward Jesus. What is His facial expression? What is His body language? What is He doing and saying?

- Ask Him, "Jesus, what truth do You want me to know about these winds and waves?"

- Ask whatever else you need to ask.

- Write down the things you see, hear, and sense.

11

JESUS CARES

$\mathcal{T}$here are many passages in God's word that make me
think, "You know, if I only had ONE scripture in my
arsenal to live by, this would be enough, Lord." Verses that are just
so profound, powerful, and practical. For me, Psalm 23 is one of
those kinds of passages. Obviously, many believers have felt that
way, too, which is probably why it is so widely known and quoted,
even by the world. Let's take a look at it.

"The Lord is my best friend and my shepherd. I always have more
than enough. He offers a resting place for me in his luxurious love.
His tracks take me to an oasis of peace, the quiet brook of bliss.
That's where he restores and revives my life. He opens before me
pathways to God's pleasure and leads me along in his footsteps of
righteousness so that I can bring honor to his name. Lord, even
when your path takes me through the valley of deepest darkness,
fear will never conquer me, for you already have! You remain close
to me and lead me through it all the way. Your authority is my
strength and my peace. The comfort of your love takes away my
fear. I'll never be lonely, for you are near. You become my delicious
feast even when my enemies dare to fight. You anoint me with the

fragrance of your Holy Spirit; you give me all I can drink of you until my heart overflows. So why would I fear the future? For your goodness and love pursue me all the days of my life. Then afterward, when my life is through, I'll return to your glorious presence to be forever with you!"

— PSALMS 23:1-6, TPT

We Are Meant For Bliss

This psalm begins with a picture of a loving shepherd watching over and guiding our life, and it ends with the idea of looking back over all of our life and seeing how He was *always* there--through every season, both good and bad, He has never abandoned us. Finally, at the conclusion of the psalm we see that we end up right where we belong and long to be—in His house, His heart, forever.

He is literally the one *leading us and following us* (having our back) *all the way through life.* Why is this truth so profound? Because sometimes life is pretty stinky. If we are going to pass through the stinky times without believing lies about ourselves or God, then we really need to intimately *know* the shepherd nature of Jesus. We need to know it, not just in our head, but in our heart.

Our Shepherd King

Jesus is so beautiful! So many precious word portraits of Him are painted in scripture. Let's focus on this one for a bit: He is our shepherd. He Himself says that He is the Good Shepherd.

"I alone am the Good Shepherd, and I know those whose hearts are mine, for they recognize me and know me, just as my Father knows my heart and I know my Father's heart. I am ready to give my life for the sheep. "And I have other sheep that I will gather which are not of this Jewish flock. And I, their shepherd, must lead them too, and they will follow me and listen to my voice. And

I will join them all into one flock with one shepherd. "The Father has an intense love for me because I freely give my own life—to raise it up again. I surrender my own life, and no one has the power to take my life from me. I have the authority to lay it down and the power to take it back again. This is the destiny my Father has set before me."

—JOHN 10:14-18, TPT

Why exactly is He a good shepherd? Because He is willing to sacrifice Himself for His sheep. When our shepherd Jesus sees us in need, His first thought isn't to send a thing, or an angel, or another person. He may indeed send all of those, but first and foremost, He gives Himself. *He comes to us in our time of need.* There is no valley too low, no mountain too steep, no sin too ugly for Him. How deeply we are loved! How deeply we are cared for!

I believe this is a truth about Jesus that satan desperately wants to keep hidden and obscured. The enemy does not want us to have a revelation of the truth of an *absolutely passionate* Jesus. Oh man, Jesus is not and never will be passive or namby-pamby about you and me. He is *the passionate pursuer of our hearts!* If one of His dear ones are lost, He searches and seeks. He leaves the ninety-nine and goes after the one. He is the man who finds the field with the buried treasure and sells *everything He has* to buy that field: "Heaven's kingdom realm can be illustrated like this: "A person discovered that there was hidden treasure in a field. Upon finding it, he hid it again. Because of uncovering such treasure, he was overjoyed and sold all that he possessed to buy the entire field just so he could have the treasure" (Matt 13:44, TPT). You are that treasure! To Him you are that one worth searching for. You are the pearl of great price to Him.

I love the beautiful revelation given to us from the Old Testament book of Ezekiel of the name of God, Jehovah Shammah. It means The Lord is There. It is only used once in scripture, and it is given as a name for the future, holy city of God—that holy city is us! This name carries the meaning of the "Overflowing Presence." Embrace that truth. Receive that picture.

One of the names of God is a revelation of His complete and eternal union with His bride, overflowing with His presence.

Wow. I am awestruck that He is so lovestruck...and *He wants us to know Him this way!*

> "...Come. I will show you the beautiful bride, the wife of the Lamb." He carried me away in the realm of the Spirit to the top of a great, high mountain. There he showed me the holy city, Jerusalem, descending out of heaven from God. It was infused with the glory of God, and its radiance was like that of a very rare jewel, like a jasper, clear as crystal."
>
> — REVELATION 21:9-11, TPT

He Gave His Treasure To Get A Treasure

> "For God has proved his love by giving us his greatest treasure, the gift of his Son. And since God freely offered him up as the sacrifice for us all, he certainly won't withhold from us anything else he has to give."
>
> — ROMANS 8:32, TPT

Here is God's heart! He is not withholding anything from us. He's not withholding things and certainly not His presence! Isn't that the great lie the enemy has perpetuated from the time of the garden of Eden until now? Satan does not want us to see and know the passionate heart of God and works to keep us out of His embrace, which is the oasis of peace and the quiet brook of bliss.

The enemy came to Eve and tempted her, but the temptation was not to merely eat a piece of fruit. *He tempted her to doubt God's heart towards her.* Sadly, she listened.

Once the seeds of doubt in God's love began to germinate within her heart, she was susceptible to sin's allure. She may have thought, "Since I can't *fully* trust that God has my best interests at heart, then I need to take care of myself." She doubted God's heart. She believed Him to be aloof and uncaring, which resulted in her choosing to meet her desires in an unhealthy way.

> "When the Woman saw that the tree looked like good eating and realized what she would get out of it—she'd know everything!—she took and ate the fruit and then gave some to her husband, and he ate."
>
> — GENESIS 3:6, MSG

Temptation's Source

There is a key here for victory over sin. The Bible teaches in James that God doesn't tempt anyone to sin (He did, after all, put the tree in the garden), but we are actually tempted to sin AFTER we are drawn away *by our own lusts and thoughts.*

> "But each one is tempted when he is carried away and enticed by his own lust. Then when lust has conceived, it gives birth to sin; and when sin is accomplished, it brings forth death."
>
> —JAMES 1:14-15, NASB

Satan's Counterfeits

Psalm 23 teaches us in verse one that we can have God's pleasure —"He leads me in the pathway to God's pleasure"(v. 1). We are created for peace and bliss in His loving presence, but the Bible also speaks of the pleasures of sin. In Hebrews 11, it says Moses chose to suffer with the people of God rather than to enjoy the pleasures of sin for a season. Sin does bring a temporary relief, fix, or thrill, but not satisfaction; it always leaves you empty and lusting for more. The short season of counterfeit pleasure that sin offers only leads to bondage to a cycle of sin, which leads to death.

Adam and Eve received death and brought forth death to all.[1] Interestingly, they were right there in the garden with that intriguing tree for some time. They didn't walk over the very first day and pick the fruit. So, what started the process that birthed sin?

- She listened to an accusation (a lie) against the heart of her Shepherd.
- She felt she could no longer trust Him to bless her and take care of her.
- She looked for other ways to get what she wanted; lust was conceived.
- Her lust led her to sin.

In my own life, if I am dealing with a temptation that seems too great to resist, there is no doubt a lie at work in my heart. If I am being drawn away over and over, then lust has been conceived in my heart and sin is likely. For example, if I believe a lie that God can't give me the affection and comfort that I need, then I will seek comfort in an unhealthy or inordinate way. This lust will lead me into any number of sin patterns including addictions, escapism, sexual promiscuity, gluttony, and more.

So, can I draw a conclusion? Yes. Having trust in the nature and love of God is ke, and the enemy is hard at work (especially at early stages of human development) to sow seeds of doubt in God's love and thus, damage our trust. From that stronghold, he will wage his war to pull us away from the fold and from the Shepherd's protection.

Try repeating this out loud, "The Lord is my shepherd. He is a good shepherd. He is willing to lay down His life for my wellbeing. Since He is willing to give His very own life, there is obviously nothing else He would withhold if I really needed it. Therefore, I shall not lust. I won't try to meet my own needs in my own way. I will choose to trust my loving Good Shepherd to give me all that I need, when I need it."

If we are living in full assurance of the love of our Shepherd as depicted in Psalm 23, then we see several amazing results.

1. I shall not want, therefore I am satisfied. I shall not lust.

2. When I need comfort and peace (green pastures, still waters), He will supply.

3. When my soul is malfunctioning, He restores it.

4. When I go through life's stinkiest of times, He is with me to guide and comfort me. I am NEVER ALONE.

5. When others may have mistreated me, He will throw me a big ol' party right in front of them, and they will be forced to watch me get His blessing. When there is warfare all around me, I can feast on the goodness of His presence and be sustained.

6. His plan for me is to live in the abundance of His anointing--so much so, that it overflows to all that surrounds me.

7. When I blow it, I don't have to run and hide because His mercy and unconditional love are always chasing me down to make me right and whole again.

8. Finally, in the end, I win, because I am a daughter or son of God living with Him forever!

Jesus Is Not Indifferent to Your Suffering

Let me share an example with you of how some healing came in my own life in this area. I grew up in poverty. I had a big family, and my father abandoned us, leaving my mother to provide for six children on her own. She worked very hard (two to three jobs at a time), but still we lacked. I don't know how this affected my other family members, but for me it was traumatic. It created a wound in my soul and a fear of lack and abandonment. I can clearly remember lying in bed at night and literally worrying myself to sleep about how we were going to make it and planning for the possibility that my family might get split up. The lie that I internalized as truth was that God was ignoring my needs. He loves me, yes, but He must not care enough about my suffering to take care of me. This lie led to a deep insecurity in my soul.

Well, I have been through some stormy waters since then, like I am sure many of you have, and I can't find even one time when God failed me. Not one. He never forsook or failed me. Not even once.

However, I still dealt with overwhelming fear for many years until He healed my wounded heart and removed the lie that said He didn't care. My healing didn't happen in one moment (although He can certainly do that), but my healing came in several touches and encounters with God. This is one of those encounters that brought me healing.

I was in India on a mission trip, and we were paying all the expenses ourselves. For a period of time, we slept on mattresses on the floor. This is not uncommon in India. I knew it wasn't my lot in life for forever. In fact, it was kind of a part of the whole "mission experience." It *should* have been fine, but my heart was experiencing a different reality.

I was feeling a deep sense of abandonment and fear. It was irrational. I had not been abandoned; I was well cared for. In fact, I had *chosen* to make the very sacrifice that was causing me such anxiety. Thankfully, I had been healed somewhat in this area of my soul and knew enough about inner healing that I was able to recognize that a lie was at work in my heart.

I went to the Lord in prayer and asked Him where this fear was coming from. He brought up a memory from years before when my husband and I were somewhat newly married and not very affluent at all. I saw myself lying on our couch and weeping because we had just received a notice that the power was going to get shut off if we didn't pay our bill. My husband was out of town. I was alone. The fearful situation took me back to my childhood trauma, and I became completely overwhelmed with fear. I laid there and wept and wept, so fearful that all I could pray was, "Jesus, please help me."

I want to say that that is a very good prayer, because we have a VERY good God! In fact, that simple, inelegant prayer has saved many souls!

As I watched this memory unfold, I realized that there were some people that I needed to forgive, starting with my husband and God. Even though they didn't do anything wrong, I still held my suffering against them. I released them. Then I asked, "Jesus, where were You?" That's when everything changed, and the hidden lie was brought into the light. Looking back at my memory, I saw Jesus come over and lay beside me on the couch. He wrapped me in His arms, and He wept with me.

I don't know if I can fully convey how deeply cared for I felt when He showed me this. I thought of Jesus's heart for me in that moment in time. He knew that everything was going to be okay. He knew the bills would be paid. He knew that there was really no reason for me to fear or to be sad. Yet I was. And He cared. So He wept with me.

Please know that your Lord is not indifferent to your suffering. He cares for you deeply. So. Deeply. The obvious Bible story that comes to mind is the story of the death of Lazarus. In this narrative, Jesus famously weeps.

"When Mary finally found Jesus outside the village, she fell at his feet in tears and said, 'Lord, if only you had been here, my brother would not have died.' When Jesus looked at Mary and saw her weeping at his feet, and all her friends who were with her grieving, he shuddered with emotion and was deeply moved with tenderness and compassion. He said to them, 'Where did you bury him?' 'Lord, come with us and we'll show you,' they replied. Then tears streamed down Jesus' face."

— JOHN 11:32-35, TPT

Jesus certainly knew that Lazarus would live again. Still He wept. He knew He was about to accomplish the greatest miracle of His earthly ministry. Still He wept. He wept because His dearest friends were sad. *This is our Jesus.* This is His personality. This is His character. This is His heart. He cares, and He cares deeply about us. We also are His dear friends.

This was the truth that my wounded heart needed in order to be healed. I can tell you also that there have been many "valley of the shadow of death" moments since then when I have pulled that image of Jesus weeping with me out of my arsenal in order to strengthen my heart. It always does. Now, I *know*. I have not merely *heard* that He cares. I don't just *believe* that He cares. I *know* it.

"The confidence of my calling enables me to overcome every difficulty without shame, for I have an intimate revelation of this God. And my faith in him convinces me that he is more than able to keep all that I've placed in his hands safe and secure until the fullness of his appearing."

— 2 TIMOTHY 1:12, TPT

When the lie gets expelled, the truth is known and embraced, and freedom is the result!

"For if you embrace the truth, it will release true freedom into your lives."

—JOHN 8:32, TPT

The Balm of Gilead was poured into that deep wound in my heart, and I was restored to wholeness in that area of my soul. This is what God wants to do for every one of us, *for every wound*. His plan is not that I have to try really hard to believe and trust and be at peace. No. John 10:10 is His intention for His friends—for His sheep.

"So Jesus said again, 'I assure you and most solemnly say to you, I am the Door for the sheep [leading to life]. All who came before Me [as false messiahs and self-appointed leaders] are thieves and robbers, but the [true] sheep did not hear them. I am the Door; anyone who enters through Me will be saved [and will live forever], and will go in and out [freely], and find pasture (spiritual security). The thief comes only in order to steal and kill and destroy. I came that they may have and enjoy life, and have it in abundance [to the full, till it overflows]. I am the Good Shepherd. The Good Shepherd lays down His [own] life for the sheep.'"

—JOHN 10:7-11, AMP

Our job is just to let Him. It's time to let God love you!

Summary

- Jesus is the Good Shepherd, and He loves us (His very own sheep) so much that He gave His own life to save us.
- We have an enemy whose mission is to separate us from our shepherd by sowing lies in our hearts about God's goodness and love.
- Temptation is a red flag that a lie is at work in my soul.
- When I am in pain, Jesus is moved with compassion. He may even weep with me. He cares for me, deeply.

- Jesus is passionate in His love!
- God intends for me to drink continually from the brooks of bliss. The river of life flows from my innermost being.
- Scriptures: Psalm 23, John 10:14-18, Romans 8:32, Genesis 3:6, James 1:14-15.

Prayer

Jesus, today I embrace You afresh and anew as my faithful, loving shepherd. I'm sorry for any times that I've doubted Your love. If I have pulled away from the fold at all. I return now fully to Your heart. I trust You to take good care of me, now and always.

Faith Declaration

"The Lord is *my* shepherd. I shall *not* want, and I lack nothing. I am meant for bliss!"

Activation

- In a time of prayer, ask the Lord to show you any time in your past when you believed that He didn't take good care of you.

- Release forgiveness to whomever you have held unforgiveness, including God.

- Take a second to pray, "Father, forgive me for doubting your faithful love. I renounce the lie that You don't passionately care for me. Father, tell me the truth…"

- Listen and receive the truth He shows you. This is your healing balm.

- Your heart wounds have His full attention. Soak in His presence and let Him love you, heal you, and fill you.

PART 3

UNVEILING TRUTH — Removing Hindrances to
Transformation

Jesus said that truth frees us.[1] By implication then, lies bind us. It is time for your freedom! Your unveiling is at hand. In fact, as each strategic, demonic lie is replaced by God's truth, you get a truer picture of Who God really is and who you really are, as well.

Are you ready to throw off those grave clothes? In this section, we are going to take some time and look at the beautiful God that we love. Get ready! He is even more lovely than you've imagined and kinder than you've thought. Let Him out of any religious "boxes" you may have put Him in, and fall more deeply in love than you ever thought possible. His unveiling is your unveiling!

A HEALTHY VIEW OF FATHER

*G*od is a father. God is a *father.* Can you picture Him in your heart as Father? Sometimes it's easier for us to relate to and connect with Jesus because He became human. Since Jesus once walked the earth like we do and experienced many of the things that we commonly do, He seems more relatable. Isn't it interesting then to recognize that one of Jesus' primary objectives when He came to earth was to *reveal* the Father!

"Philip spoke up, 'Lord, show us the Father, and that will be all that we need!' Jesus replied, 'Philip, I've been with you all this time and you still don't know who I am? How could you ask me to show you the Father, for anyone who has looked at me has seen the Father. Don't you believe that the Father is living in me and that I am living in the Father? Even my words are not my own but come from my Father, for he lives in me and performs his miracles of power through me. Believe that I live as one with my Father and that my Father lives as one with me—or at least, believe because of the mighty miracles I have done. I tell you this timeless truth: The person who follows me in faith, believing in me, will do the same mighty miracles that I do—even greater miracles than these because I go to be with my Father! For I will do whatever you ask me to do when you ask me in my name. And that is how the Son will show what the Father is really like and bring glory to him. Ask me anything in my name, and I will do it for you!'"

—John 14:8-14, TPT

Jesus wants us to know His dad! He is pretty passionate about that. He laid down His own life in order to restore us to the Father.

"Jesus explained, 'I am the Way, I am the Truth, and I am the Life. No one comes next to the Father except through union with me. To know me is to know my Father too. And from now on you will realize that you have seen him and experienced him'"

—John 14:6-7, TPT

The Godhead Exists in an Embrace

Jesus left the embrace of God in order to bring us into that same embrace!

"In the very beginning the Living Expression (Jesus) was already there. And the Living Expression was with God, yet fully God. They were together— face-to-face, in the very beginning.

He entered into the very world he created, yet the world was unaware. He came to the very people he created— to those who should have recognized him, but they did not receive him. But those who embraced him and took hold of his name were given authority to become the children of God!

No one has ever gazed upon the fullness of God's splendor except the uniquely beloved Son, who is cherished by the Father and held close to his heart. Now he has unfolded to us the full explanation of who God truly is!"

—John 1:1-2, 10-12, 18, TPT, insert added

"So my Father, restore me back to the glory that we shared together when we were face-to-face before the universe was created."

—JOHN 17:5, TPT

Father And Son

We can see some beautiful aspects of Father God's personality and heart by studying the way He treated the Son. The dynamics of their relationship can be seen in the words and interactions that they shared. The picture that is painted by their relationship shows us what is available to us as well, because after all, we are His kids, too!

Here are just a few vignettes of Father from the Bible:

"Didn't you know I had to be about my father's business?"
"I and the Father are one."
"This is my Son. Listen to Him!"
"Thank you for hearing me. I know that You always hear me."
"Not My will but Your will be done."
"Abba, if there is any other way, let this cup pass from me."
"This is My beloved Son in whom I am well pleased."

The word *abba* is an Aramaic word that would most closely be translated as the English word, daddy. It was a common name that small children would use to address their fathers. The word abba so sweetly illustrates the close, intimate relationship of a father to his child, as well as the childlike trust that a young child puts in his daddy. God is Father to Jesus, but He is also Daddy. *He is our daddy, too!*

It is significant that the only place in scripture where Jesus used this intimate term of endearment, Abba, was during His darkest hour. This blesses me so! When it seems that the world is crashing down on us, we can cry out to Abba. When everyone else has left us high and dry, Abba will come running. Whether I am in the highest heights of success or the deepest depths of despair, Abba is there. In my greatest successes or my worst failures, He is my dad. That is who He is.

A father, in the natural, is a person who meets (or is intended to meet) specific needs in a child's life. A father is intended to be: provider, protector, and identifier. Let's look at how Father God met those needs for Jesus.

Provider

One example of Father as provider was in the gifts that the Magi brought to Jesus. It was certainly not a very auspicious beginning for One meant to be a king, was it? Born in a manger, in obscurity and poverty, He came without pomp or circumstance...except for the wise men. Some stories just don't need much commentary, do they? Yes, wise men do still seek Him. These wise men went on the journey of all journeys to worship the King of all Kings.

They also came bearing gifts. If you read between the lines in this beautiful story, you see that these costly gifts were delivered at a very strategic moment for this vulnerable, poor, and lonely family. Joseph, Mary, and toddler Jesus were given these treasures literally in the nick of time. Mere days later, they escaped the clutches of King Herod and fled to Egypt. The gifts of the Magi likely funded their years spent in a foreign land without family, friends, or home.

Just as Father provided for Jesus, He also takes very good care of us! We are called to a life of prayer, one aspect of which is *asking*. When we simply ask Father God, He never fails to answer. The answer may at times be different than we expect, but it will always be best. Look at these beautiful encouraging verses about Father God, the provider.

> "So it is with your prayers. Ask and you'll receive. Seek and you'll discover. Knock on heaven's door, and it will one day open for you. Every persistent person will get what he asks for. Every persistent

seeker will discover what he needs. And everyone who knocks persistently will one day find an open door.

Let me ask you this: Do you know of any father who would give his son a snake on a plate when he asked for a serving of fish? Of course not! Do you know of any father who would give his daughter a spider when she had asked for an egg? Of course not! If imperfect parents know how to lovingly take care of their children and give them what they need, how much more will the perfect heavenly Father give the Holy Spirit's fullness when his children ask him."

— Luke 11:9-13, TPT

"When you pray, there is no need to repeat empty phrases, praying like those who don't know God, for they expect God to hear them because of their many words. There is no need to imitate them, since your Father already knows what you need before you ask him. Pray like this: 'Our Father, dwelling in the heavenly realms, may the glory of your name be the center on which our lives turn. Manifest your kingdom realm, and cause your every purpose to be fulfilled on earth, just as it is fulfilled in heaven. We acknowledge you as our Provider of all we need each day."

— Matthew 6:7-11, TPT

Protector

One place in scripture where we see Father God as Jesus's protector is actually in the Garden of Gethsemane. More specifically, we see it in Jesus's prayer.

"He was saying, 'Abba, Father! All things are possible for You; take this cup [of judgment] away from Me; but not what I will, but what You will…'"

— Mark 14:36, AMP

What I see when I read this cry from the heart of Jesus is His *complete confidence* in His Father's power and love to protect Him. The only question for Jesus was if there might be another way. In other words, He was asking, "Dad, is there another way we could do this?" He settles His question the same way we must always settle ours, which was "...not what I will, but what You will..." The Father's will on the matter of Jesus's suffering had actually already been written hundreds of years earlier through the prophet Isaiah:

> "Yet the LORD was *willing* to crush Him, causing Him to suffer; If He would give Himself as a guilt offering [an atonement for sin], He shall see His [spiritual] offspring, He shall prolong His days, And the will (good pleasure) of the LORD shall succeed and prosper in His hand..."
>
> — ISAIAH 53:10, AMP, EMPHASIS ADDED

In this very dark and difficult moment of Jesus's earthly life, we see Jesus *never* doubting Father's heart or His love. In fact, He was so confident in that love that He boldly asked a *huge* request. Jesus knew the Bible. He knew what had been foretold. He simply believed so completely in the love of the Father that He asked for the moon! I personally feel that Jesus believed His Dad could possibly rewrite the whole plan. So He asked! *Three times.* He asked. He asked again. Then He asked again. Are you getting the picture here? *This is relationship.* Jesus had unshakable confidence in His Dad's desire and ability to protect Him from harm. *We can have that same confidence.*

> "His massive arms are wrapped around you, protecting you. You can run under his covering of majesty and hide. His arms of faithfulness are a shield keeping you from harm."
>
> — PSALMS 91:4, TPT

Identifier

We see Father God identify Jesus *undeniably* at His baptism.

> "And as Jesus rose up out of the water, the heavenly realm opened up over him and he saw the Holy Spirit descend out of the heavens and rest upon him in the form of a dove. Then suddenly the voice of the Father shouted from the sky, saying, 'This is the Son I love, and my greatest delight is in him.'"

> — MATTHEW 3:16-17, TPT

There are many, many, words that the Father could have said about His Son (worthy and true words), but He said only what was necessary, *"You're mine, and I love you so!"*

As it was true for Jesus, it is also true for each one of us. If you have been identified as a most beloved child, all the things that God has planned for you to accomplish will naturally flow from the confidence and security of the Father's pleasure in *who you are*. His pleasure doesn't come "from your do" but rather "from your who." He also is speaking this message over you: "You are my beloved child. In you, I am *well pleased*."

The Vastness of the Father's Heart

Over the past few years, we have had a lot of good teaching in the Church exposing the orphan heart and helping the body of Christ to recognize unhealthy striving and performing that comes from a need to earn love and acceptance from Father God. This has been necessary exposure of a wrong mindset and theology, but we need more than just a diagnosis, don't we? We need the remedy! The remedy for a wounded or orphaned heart is very simple: *the embrace of God*. In that intimate, life giving connection, we are continually healed. Orphans become sons in His healing presence.

According to Psalm 139, we interfaced with God before we were even born. He knew us. He planned us and planned *for* us. He dreamed the dream of *you* and recorded it in the book of your life. You are known by God, and you will only find true peace in relationship with Him. We often hear the saying that there is a God-shaped hole in every human heart, and this is poignantly true. When we come into His embrace, we are truly coming home!

It is also true, however, that there is a you-shaped hole within the Father's heart. Oh yes! You are wanted, with great passion. If that seems too good to be true, or a little "out there" to you, then you likely really need to hear this truth! *You are special to God!*

I grew up in a family of six children. We were often in lack and without a father. I had a deep longing to feel special, a longing that could have been filled in a loving father-daughter connection, but wasn't. I came into my relationship with the Lord with that longing, and, to my delight, found out something wonderful and life-changing that I'd like to share with you.

I was in prayer one day early in my walk with the Lord, and that very familiar desire kept bubbling up in my heart: a desire to be special. Finally, I poured out my heart and longing for this to the Lord, and He answered my need with this beautiful declaration. He said, "Teresa, nobody loves me the way that you do."

Can you receive that amazing truth today into your own heart? You are cherished in the heart of God. You are not just one of the many people in His big people collection. No, you are unique and uniquely loved. You are special. You are His delight and you satisfy Him with your love. Jesus taught us this truth in John 14.

> "My Father's house has many dwelling places. If it were otherwise, I would tell you plainly, because I go to prepare a place for you to rest. And when everything is ready, I will come back and take you to myself so that you will be where I am..."

> —JOHN 14:2-3, TPT

We are each a dwelling place of God. He makes His home within each of our hearts. God no longer dwells in a man-made temple. He dwells in us, His church! But there is more—we are His home, and *He is ours!* Jesus said to us, "I go to prepare a place for you to rest, so that you will be where I am." Friends, where is Jesus? He is in the embrace of God.

> "They were together— face-to-face, in the very beginning."
>
> —John 1:2, TPT

Our *place*, the place He has prepared for us through His blood sacrifice, is also in the *embrace of the Father!*

This is why the Son came! He came from the embrace of God in order to bring us into that same divine hug! And, we find there, complete rest, the true rest that we have always longed for since the beginning, when He first formed us.

> "No one has ever gazed upon the fullness of God's splendor. But if we love one another, God makes his permanent home in us, and we make our permanent home in him, and his love is brought to its full expression in us. And he has given us his Spirit within us so that we can have the assurance that he lives in us and that we live in him."
>
> — 1 John 4:12-13, TPT

Put simply, He is our home AND we are His home. This is not just meant collectively as the Church, but individually. Jesus said it plainly and truly, "Within My Father's house, there are many dwelling places." You are one of those places! No one—no matter how lovely, gifted, or great—can take that place. Indeed, no one can love Him the way you do.

> "For here is eternal truth: When that time comes you won't need to ask me for anything, but instead you will go directly to the

Father and ask him for anything you desire and he will give it to you, because of your relationship with me. Until now you've not been bold enough to ask the Father for a single thing in my name, but now you can ask, and keep on asking him! And you can be sure that you'll receive what you ask for, and your joy will have no limits! 'I have spoken to you using figurative language, but the time is coming when I will no longer teach you with veiled speech, but I will teach you about the Father with your eyes unveiled. And I will not need to ask the Father on your behalf, for you'll ask him directly because of your new relationship with me. For the Father tenderly loves you, because you love me and believe that I've come from God. I came to you sent from the Father's presence, and I entered into the created world, and now I will leave this world and return to the Father's side.'"

—JOHN 16:23-28, TPT

The Trust Factor

All the success stories of the Bible are really stories of one person's great *relationship* with God Almighty, not their great *ability*. Their success ultimately is the result of their *face to face conversations with Father.*

Abraham failed, Isaac failed, Jacob failed, Moses failed, David failed, Peter failed... So then why are all these individuals all considered spiritual giants and faith "hall of famers"? The answer, I believe, is trust.

Faith is powerful, necessary, a mountain-mover and miracle manifester. However, *trust is the love factor that makes everything work right in a relationship.*

I have heard it said that trust is God's love language, and I so believe this is true! *Our trusting heart melts His!* Our trusting prayers move Him to act. Our childlike trust (not presumption but spirit and truth, worshipful, and loving reliance) is the pen that writes our history with God.

*Faith moves mountains—trust
moves the mountain-Maker!*

Lifting, Propping, Pruning

> "I am a true sprouting vine, and *the farmer who tends the vine is my Father.* He cares for the branches connected to me by lifting and propping up the fruitless branches and pruning every fruitful branch to yield a greater harvest."
>
> —JOHN 15:1-2, TPT, EMPHASIS ADDED

Father God is the husbandman of our life! Jesus gave us this one-of-a-kind portrait of The Father in John fifteen. He showed us a loving vinedresser (farmer) who actually gets on his knees in the dirt with us in order to lift us up, prop us up, and prune us for a fuller abundance and blessing in life. He is not aloof and far off! He is invested in our lives.

A vinedresser, or husbandman, is more than a mere farmer. Grapes are more than an annual crop. The vinedresser's grape vines remain with him for *decades.* He comes to know each one in a personal way, much like a shepherd with his sheep. He knows how the vine is faring from year to year and which ones are more productive or vigorous than others. He knows what they respond to and what special care certain one's need. Every vine has its own personality, and the vinedresser comes to know it over the years.[1]

The vinedresser cares for each vine and nurtures it, pruning it the appropriate amount at the appropriate times, fertilizing it, lifting its branches from the ground and propping them or tying them to the trellis, and taking measures to protect them from insects and disease.

I have studied the ancient tool that grape farmers would have used in the time of Christ, and it gives a fascinating picture. The ancient pruning tool was called a *falx vinitoria,* and it was like the Swiss Army knife of gardening tools! It could perform multiple functions, but what really struck me was how intricately it had to be utilized. It was made in such a way where the farmer must take it one branch at a time, bit by bit. It was basically an art!

Isn't that just how tenderly Father deals with us? Aren't you glad He doesn't come to a group of His kids with a broad and fearsome scythe and just start swinging, dealing with us all together without specialized care? I know I am! I am so glad that He is like the gentle farmer Jesus described, who lovingly lifts, props, and prunes us for our good and for His pleasure. He is indeed a *good, good* Father.

Summary

- We can get an accurate picture of the Father's heart by studying Jesus. Jesus is His exact representation in the earth.
- We can learn how Father wants to protect, provide for, and identify us by studying how He did those things for our big brother, Jesus.
- Father is our provider, protector, and source of identity.
- The embrace of God heals the orphan heart.
- Jesus and Father were face to face from the beginning.
- Jesus came to bring us into the embrace of God.
- Scriptures for further study: John 1:1-18, John 14-15, John 16:23-28, Matthew 3:16-17

Prayer

Father, thank You for being Father to me. I haven't always had a good earthly father experience, but I am grateful that You love me better. I choose to forgive my earthly dad for in any way that he hurt or failed me. I ask You to heal those wounds, Lord. I release my earthly dad from any harm that he caused me know-

ingly or unknowingly. I release him, and I bless him in Jesus's mighty name. I no longer will accuse or label my dad, but instead, I choose to cover his faults and failures, shortcomings and sins, great and small, with love. Father, I ask You to bring me into a greater intimacy with You than I could have ever imagined. I want to know You more! Amen.

Faith Declaration

"There is a 'me' shaped hole in the Father's heart that nobody else could ever fill. I am irreplaceable and uniquely loved in my daddy's heart."

Activation

- During a time of prayer, take a moment and picture Father God.

- Get as close as you can to Him. Climb right up onto His lap.

- Ask the Father, "Father, is there any lie I'm believing about You? What truth do You want me to know about Your love? Father, what do You think of me?"

- Write down what you see, hear, and sense.

A HEALTHY VIEW OF JESUS

*T*here are not enough words to describe Him! The songwriter Charles Wesley said it this way, "Oh! For a thousand tongues to sing my great Redeemer's praise!" Really, He *is* beautiful beyond description, is He not? In the Gospel of John, it says that the world couldn't contain all the books that could be written telling of all He is and has done.

So let's focus on a few portraits of Jesus that I believe help to bring healing and greater intimacy with Him. Scripture paints a portrait of Jesus as friend and brother.

The natural family relationship that correlates to our relationship with Jesus is the sibling relationship and close friendships.[1] If we had good connections with siblings and close friends, then we will have an easier time connecting with Jesus. If those earthly bonds were not great, or if they were damaged by betrayal, abuse, or rejection, then we may be harboring some lies in our souls that hinder our deeper connection with Jesus. Let's expose some lies.

What A Friend We Have In Jesus

JESUS WOULD NEVER BETRAY US. In fact, He did the exact opposite when He laid down His life for us!

> "For the greatest love of all is a love that sacrifices all. And this great love is demonstrated when a person sacrifices his life for his friends."
>
> —JOHN 15:13, TPT

JESUS DOESN'T KEEP SECRETS FROM US. In fact, He shares His secrets with us!

> "I have never called you 'servants,' because a master doesn't confide in his servants, and servants don't always understand what the master is doing. But I call you my most intimate friends, for I reveal to you everything that I've heard from my Father."
>
> —JOHN 15:15, TPT

JESUS WANTS US TO SUCCEED; HE IS NEVER TRYING TO PUT US OR PUSH US DOWN. In fact, He wants to bring us up alongside Himself!

> "A pupil is not superior to his teacher, but everyone [when he is] completely trained (readjusted, restored, set to rights, and perfected) will be like his teacher."
>
> — LUKE 6:40, AMPC

JESUS IS NOT TREATING US LIKE STEP-SIBLINGS AND OUTSIDERS. In fact, He wants us to be just as close to His Dad as He is!

> "For the very glory you have given to me I have given them so that they will be joined together as one and experience the same unity that we enjoy. You live fully in me and now I live fully in them so

that they will experience perfect unity, and the world will be convinced that you have sent me, for they will see that you love each one of them with the same passionate love that you have for me. Father, I ask that you allow everyone that you have given to me to be with me where I am! Then they will see my full glory— the very splendor you have placed upon me because you have loved me even before the beginning of time. You are my righteous Father, but the unbelieving world has never known you in the perfect way that I know you! And all those who believe in me also know that you have sent me! I have revealed to them who you are and I will continue to make you even more real to them, so that they may experience the same endless love that you have for me, for your love will now live in them, even as I live in them!"

—JOHN 17:22-26, TPT

This passage of scripture was a portion of Jesus's final prayer for His friends. You can see here that Jesus wants *the very best* for His friends. That is the kind of friend He is!

Jesus Is Not Boring

During prayer ministry times, I often see a beautiful phenomenon. When Jesus reveals Himself to hearts, He frequently reveals Himself as (wait for it) a *fun guy!* I am truly sorry if this is offensive to anyone reading this. I realize it could possibly be a jarring thought to someone who has never really thought of Jesus that way. I believe He wants us to know Him fully, and I humbly submit that Jesus is adventurous, funny, endearing, and kind of wild (in a good way)!

"And so the Living Expression became a man and lived among us! And we gazed upon the splendor of his glory, the glory of the One and Only who came from the Father overflowing with tender mercy and truth! John taught the truth about him when he announced to the people, "He's the One! Set your hearts on him! I told you he would come after me, even though he ranks far above me, for he existed before I was even born." And now out of his fullness we are fulfilled! And from him we receive grace heaped upon more grace! Moses gave us the Law, but Jesus, the Anointed One, unveils truth wrapped in tender mercy."

—John 1:14-17, TPT

Jesus came to unveil truth, but not on stone tablets through a law that wounds. No, He came to heal us with truth *wrapped in tender mercy!*

> ### *Jesus came as a message wrapped in delight, joy, and splendor.*

That is who He is! He came to fulfill our hearts! How? Out of His fullness. He wants to bless our spiritual socks off, not bore us into spiritual comas.

One depiction of this is seen in the very first miracle Jesus performed. He turned water into wine at a wedding celebration. Come on! What a beautiful revelation to us that Jesus came to bring fullness and life. He turns the empty, stone pots of religion into over-flowing vats of the wine of His love and glory. And, it was a WEDDING! He began His love message to us at a wedding and wraps things up in the book of Revelation at the wedding supper of the Lamb. Goodness, but how He longs for intimacy and oneness with each one of us! The plan is truly fullness, and so we can declare what John the Baptist said, "He's the One! Set your hearts on Him!"

Throw out the old pictures of Jesus from some outdated movie where He *never smiles,* never shows hardly *any emotion,* and acts *boring.*

That ain't Jesus! He thinks *big!* He dreams *big!* He picked you, didn't He? He is obviously looking for adventure!

The Best Big Brother... *Ever!*

Maybe you are blessed with great sibling relationships. I hope so. But at the same time, I know that the reality is that many of us were not. Perhaps your earthly brothers or sisters mistreated or ignored you. Possibly they were jealous of the attention you took away from them and felt the need to push you down or put you down. Maybe there was even verbal, emotional, physical, or sexual abuse. Sadly, this is the case in many families.

Satan targets the family unit because a healthy family is *so powerful.* A healthy home is meant to be a little piece of heaven on earth. God Himself is, after all, essentially a family (consisting of a Father, Son, and Spirit)! He wanted to grow His family and dreamed us up! We were a precious dream in the heart of God, and He is making His dream a reality every single day!

> "Jesus continued, 'In the same way, there will be a glorious celebration in heaven over the rescue of one lost sinner who repents, comes back home, and returns to the fold—more so than for all the righteous people who never strayed away.'"
>
> — LUKE 15:7, TPT

This verse actually says that heaven celebrates. Can you picture that celebration? God Himself celebrates when a sinner repents. The word for celebrate there is *chara* and it means *joy* and *delight.* It also means "grace recognized," meaning that when the grace of God is seen in our lives, heaven celebrates![2] I love that thought!

Once we come into right relationship with God, many times some healing needs to take place in this area of woundedness from family failings. So, I wanted to take a bit of time and focus on Jesus as the *ultimate* brother.

First of all, we do know that in the natural Jesus was a big brother. Some Bible scholars think Jesus may have been one of seven children in the Mary and Joseph household—yes, *seven!* We do know for sure that He had at least four brothers and at least two sisters.

> "Isn't he just the wood-worker's son? Isn't his mother named Mary, and his four brothers Jacob, Joseph, Simon, and Judah? And don't his sisters all live here in Nazareth? How did he get all this revelation and power?"
>
> — MATTHEW 13:55-56, TPT

Let me paint the picture here. Jesus had at least 6 younger siblings! Times were different 2,000 years ago, no doubt... but not *that* different.

So, big brother Jesus would have likely wiped noses, cleaned up messes (hey, no pampers back then), washed owies, combed hair, gave baths, broke up skirmishes, gave advice, scared off bad suitors, gave a stern talking to when needed, wiped away tears, helped with homework, probably sighed and shook His headed a few times, kissed boo boos, and more! Are you getting a mental picture yet?

How about this... He also likely played in the dirt, fished with his little brothers, built forts, played some version of cops and robbers, used pretend voices when playing with little sisters, helped to learn sports and games, cheered from the sidelines, danced with His sisters, showed His sisters how gentlemen behave, and became the father figure when Joseph passed away.

Jesus is our brother, too, and He is the best! I promise you, if Jesus had been your brother, He would have *treasured you!* And now, because you have been adopted into His family, He *is* your brother. *He does treasure You!*

> "And today GOD has reaffirmed that you are dearly held treasure just as he promised, a people entrusted with keeping his commandments, a people set high above all other nations that he's

made, high in praise, fame, and honor: you're a people holy to GOD, your God. That's what he has promised."

— DEUTERONOMY 26:18-19, MSG

Is your heart singing right now with a new song? Are you captivated with the beauty of Jesus? Are you ready to begin making a deeper connection with Him? That would make His day!

(Jesus is also our heavenly Bridegroom, which we will talk more about in future chapters.)

Summary

- Jesus is our friend.
- As a friend, Jesus is a good listener, He is rooting for us, and He is excited about our accomplishments, successes, and plans.
- Jesus wants to do life with us. He is adventurous, spontaneous, and fun-loving.
- Jesus is *never* boring.
- Jesus is our brother, our big brother.
- Jesus is the Son of God, but He is also called the Son of Man.[3] He understands us in our humanity. He gets it.
- As our big brother, Jesus *celebrates and treasures us.* He is our biggest fan!

Prayer

Jesus, I really like You! You are the best! I love You! You make my heart happy. Nobody thrills me like You do. You are with me in the valleys, but You are also with me in the high times. You are the friend that really does stick closer than a brother. Lord Jesus, help me to be a good friend to You as well. Help me to walk with You and talk with You, and to know You more. I welcome and look forward to all the adventures that lie ahead of us. Bring it on! I believe I can do all things with Your strength, hand in hand with You, so let's go for it! Because of Your love and grace, I choose to move forward unafraid. Amen.

Faith Declaration

"God has *chosen* me and adopted me into His family... I am one of the family!"

Activation

- In your time alone with God take a moment and picture Jesus. What does He look like? What is He wearing, doing, and saying?

- Ask Him, "Jesus, is there any lie that I'm believing about You?"

- Ask, "What truth do You want me to know about You?"

- Try asking, "What do You think of me?"

- Ask this of Him, "What truth do You want me to know about my future?"

- Be sure to write down what you see, hear, and feel.

14

A HEALTHY VIEW OF HOLY SPIRIT

he Holy Spirit is possibly the most overlooked member of the trinity. Often, He is even referred to as an "it." But, oh, the joy that comes to the heart of one who discovers Him as a *person*, real and ever-present.

> "Because you are close to me and always available, my confidence will never be shaken, for I experience your wrap-around presence every moment."
>
> — PSALMS 16:8 TPT

The Fellowship of the Spirit

Paul, the apostle, prays for believers that we may have the communion of the Holy Spirit.

> "Now, may the grace and joyous favor of the Lord Jesus Christ, the unambiguous love of God, and the precious communion that we share in the Holy Spirit be yours continually. Amen!"
>
> — 2 CORINTHIANS 13:14, TPT

Communion carries the meaning of the sharing of deep thoughts and feelings. It connotes intimate fellowship. Fellowship means companionship, company, the company of equals or friends, friendship, and mutual support.

When Jesus was on the earth, as He was trying to prepare His disciples for His departure, He basically said to them, "Look, if you knew who was coming to replace me, you would be ecstatic! If I don't go, then He can't come! I've been here walking *with* you, but He will be *in* you!" Take notice of how passionate He was about sending Holy Spirit to be our closest companion.

> "But here's the truth: It's to your advantage that I go away, for if I don't go away the Divine Encourager will not be released to you. But after I depart, I will send him to you.
>
> There is so much more I would like to say to you, but it's more than you can grasp at this moment. But when the truth-giving Spirit comes, he will unveil the reality of every truth within you. He won't speak on his own, but only what he hears from the Father, and he will reveal prophetically to you what is to come."
>
> —JOHN 16:7, 12-13, TPT

> "And I will ask the Father and he will give you another Savior, the Holy Spirit of Truth, who will be to you a friend just like me—and he will never leave you. The world won't receive him because they can't see him or know him. But you know him intimately because he remains with you and will live inside you."
>
> —JOHN 14:16-17, TPT

Let's explore the personality of the Holy Spirit, whom Jesus was so excited to send to be our divine encourager. These are just a few of the traits we see in the scriptures above:

- Advocate

- Comforter
- Intercessor
- Helper
- Strengthener
- Standby
- Teacher
- Guide
- Spirit of Truth

This speaks to me clearly that, as a part of the Godhead, there are some very important needs in our life that Holy Spirit is meant to supply. As we talked about previously, when we don't let God meet our needs, we *will* try to meet those needs in another way (usually a substandard way) that may lead us into bondage.

One example of this that I am going to share is in regards to our need for comfort. The Holy Spirit is so kind and gentle. More than once, during times of prayer ministry for inner healing, the person praying will see Holy Spirit as a warm, lush blanket that is wrapped around them completely. They feel safe, covered, nurtured, and peaceful.

This is *so* His heart for us! Just look at these short definitions and realize that they describe the ministry of the Spirit in our lives.

Comfort: the easing or alleviation of a person's feelings of grief or distress.[1]

Communion: the sharing or exchanging of intimate thoughts and feelings, especially when the exchange is on a mental or spiritual level.[2]

Consolation: a person or thing providing comfort to a person who has suffered.[3]

Lies Can Block Our Connection to Holy Spirit

One particular ministry session encounter revealed a perfect example of what can happen when things go wrong in the mother-child relationship. The mother and child relationship in the natural family is the earthly family model of the heavenly family relationship between Holy Spirit and believer.[4]

If moms fail us (and they will because they are human), then very often this disappointment will leak over into our view of Holy Spirit. This causes us to doubt His ability or desire to meet our needs (for comfort, help, guidance, etc.). This sets us up to look for other (false and empty) comforters.

> "My people have committed two sins: They have forsaken me, the spring of living water, and have dug their own cisterns, broken cisterns that cannot hold water."
>
> —JEREMIAH 2:13, NIV

If, in unbelief, we don't come to Holy Spirit for fulfillment, we may turn aside to cracked pots that can't satisfy.

During this particular ministry time that I referenced, the young man we were praying with was seeking a closer connection with Holy Spirit, and He was having a hard time breaking through. There was a blockage, and the Lord brought a memory of a childhood experience to his mind that was the root cause of the problem.

He remembered a time when he was young and had been very sick. Now, we all get the sniffles occasionally, but this illness had been *miserable* for him. He had felt pain throughout his little body and just laid in the basement family room of their home on a couch in agony of pain, fever, and chills.

He remembered *clearly* how alone he felt. He also remembered how his mom essentially ignored him and left him to himself until he recovered. Obviously, she had some issues herself, because this is not normal mom behavior. So, he had to forgive her. He also needed to renounce the lie that Holy Spirit would ever just ignore his needs. This was the lie that He internalized as the truth about relating to Holy Spirit.

Here are some examples of other lies that can take root:

- Mother was controlling - Spirit is controlling.
- Mother was too busy - Spirit is unavailable.
- Mother was weak and needy - Spirit is not strong and reliable.
- Mother was domineering - Spirit is harsh and scary.
- Mother embarrassed me - Spirit will humiliate me.
- Mother was intolerant - Spirit is hard to please.
- Mother was cold and distant - Spirit is distant and difficult to connect with.
- Mother resented me - Spirit doesn't want me.

At this point, he remembered something very significant that he had completely forgotten about until that very moment during his ministry time. This is *very* common, by the way. Once forgiveness is released, it is as if things simply become unlocked. He saw in the memory that his mom had come at one point during his sickness. She had opened the doors at the top of the stairs and tossed him a blanket. She then shut the doors again.

At that very moment in his aloneness and pain, a demonic spirit came and offered him comfort. He didn't share with the prayer team in what form that comfort was offered, nor did we ask. It didn't really matter. It could have been self-pity, fantasy, addiction, escapism (in movies, books, games, tv, internet, etc.), masturbation, rejection, or any number of other *false comforters*. The important truth is that it was a *counterfeit*.

He renounced it, repented, and gave it to the Lord. I bet you can guess what God gave Him in exchange! *The* Comforter came to comfort him—the intimate Nurturer, who will never fail to meet our deepest needs for care and comfort.

Holy Spirit is the warm blanket
of God's presence
that never leaves us cold.

Covered By Glory

A study of the songs and prayers of David contained in the book of Psalms reveals amazing insight into the victory keys that David held. He yielded those victory keys through his many dark moments of accusation, slander, betrayal, and warfare. He was a man of war, yes. But he was also a man of prayer, and an intimate worshipper. He knew where to run in times of trouble. He did not run to man, nor to a fortress, or a man-made refuge. He ran to the embrace of God. That was His safe place, his shelter, his place of victory. From that place, hidden in God's arms and covered in the blanket of God's glory, he fought his battles.

That is where we have the victory as well! Like David, we can acknowledge the lies and flaming arrows of the enemy, but then tuck ourselves into God's presence like a child and say, "But this is what I truly know."

> "But in the depths of my heart I truly know that you, Yahweh, have become my Shield; You take me and surround me with yourself. Your glory covers me continually. You lift high my head when I bow low in shame. I have cried out to you, Yahweh, from your holy presence. You send me a Father's help."
>
> — PSALMS 3:3-4, TPT

From that place, seated with Him in the glory realm, we fight our battles. We call upon our champion God, and He sends a Father's help as we abide cocooned in the blanket of His love.

The glory of God is His weighty presence. Science has shown that people who suffer from anxiety get relief from something called weighted blanket therapy. A heavy blanket covers them and their panic, stress, and anxiety greatly diminishes. Wow! We are indeed created for the glory of God. Adam and Eve lost that continual glory covering, receiving instead a poor substitute of fig leaves. Fig leaves represent the religious effort of man, and it falls so short of the glory of God. However, we have now been restored through Christ! No poor substitutes for us! No. We receive and embrace the precious Holy Spirit in and upon us in fullness.

A Mighty Rushing Wind

Holy Spirit is gentle. He is never pushy and abrasive. He doesn't go where He is not invited. In fact, He is a gentleman. But make no mistake, He is no wimp. When we invite Him, He comes! And when He comes, He brings all the power of heaven with Him.

> "On the day Pentecost was being fulfilled, all the disciples were gathered in one place. Suddenly they heard the sound of a violent blast of wind rushing into the house from out of the heavenly realm. The roar of the wind was so overpowering it was all anyone could bear! Then all at once a pillar of fire appeared before their eyes. It separated into tongues of fire that engulfed each one of them. They were all filled and equipped with the Holy Spirit and were inspired to speak in tongues—empowered by the Spirit to speak in languages they had never learned!"
>
> — Acts 2:1-4, TPT

He sure came, *with power.* When we ask for Him to come, He will not ignore us, put us off, or be too busy. Sometimes moms (or teachers) will do those things, but Holy Spirit *never will.* That doesn't mean that we may not have to wait on His perfect timing, but it does mean that He *will always come,* and He is worth the wait!

Give the Invitation

I have been a Christian now for several years, but for the first twelve years I didn't really know Holy Spirit very well. I ignored Him, not knowing how much I needed His help and strength and guidance. I also didn't walk in much victory because I was trying to walk in my own power. I didn't know how available Holy Spirit was to me! Once I opened my heart and life to Him, He immediately accepted my invitation. I am *so grateful* that He did. My life has never been the same. I want to encourage you to extend an invitation to Him as well. He won't disappoint you.

> "For John baptized you in water, but in a few days from now you will be baptized in the Holy Spirit! Every time they were gathered together, they asked Jesus, 'Lord, is it the time now for you to free Israel and restore our kingdom?' He answered, 'The Father is the one who sets the fixed dates and the times of their fulfillment. You are not permitted to know the timing of all that he has prepared by his own authority. But I promise you this—the Holy Spirit will come upon you and you will be seized with power. And you will be my messengers to Jerusalem, throughout Judea, the distant provinces—even to the remotest places on earth!'"
>
> — Acts 1:5-8, TPT

Summary

- Holy Spirit is the One who walks with us in this earth.
- He is our helper, comforter, teacher, counselor, guide, and companion.
- Holy Spirit will meet our *deepest longings* for consolation and comfort. He will *never* fail at this.
- The Holy Spirit is not content to be ignored—He wants us!
- Holy Spirit is gentle, sweet, kind, *and* powerful!
- He awaits our invitation to come.
- Scriptures for deeper study: John 14:16-17; John 16:7,12-

13; 2 Corinthians 13:14; Jeremiah 2:13; Psalms 3:3-4; Acts 1:5-8; Acts 2:1-4

Prayer

Father, I receive Your promise of the Holy Spirit. I know He will never ignore me (my cries, my needs, or my wants), and I repent for any way that I have ignored Him. Holy Spirit come! I want You. I need You. I make room for You in my life. I invite You to walk with me through this life, hand in hand, heart to heart. Comfort me, Holy Spirit, teach me, lead me into all truth. You are the Spirit of truth. Jesus, please baptize me with the Holy Spirit and fire so that I may be Your witness in the earth, with power. I receive You, Holy Spirit. I welcome You into every nook and cranny of my life, every room in my heart. Have Your way in me. Come with Your mighty rushing wind and make any changes You want. I want to be a vessel that You can fill and use. Holy Spirit, in this adventure called life, You are my partner and guide, so let's do this! Amen.

Faith Declaration

"Holy Spirit, You are *so very* welcome in my life."

Activation

- Set aside some time alone with God. Picture Holy Spirit and snuggle up to Him as close as you can. Soak in His love.

- Say to Him, "Holy Spirit, is there any lie I am believing about You? Holy Spirit, what truth do You want me to know about You? What do You think of Me?" and any other questions that come to your heart.

- Be sure to write down what He speaks and reveals.

- If you sense a wall and it is difficult to enter into communion with Holy Spirit, ask the Lord to reveal to you what the block is. Begin by forgiving your mom. Remember, admitting that your mom made mistakes does not make her evil or the bad guy. It is not dishonoring to her to recognize how she may have hurt or failed you. Forgive her, and renounce the lie that Holy Spirit is capable of hurting you or failing you in that way.

THREE THINGS YOU CANNOT REPENT OF

*R*epentance is absolutely a powerful part of walking in freedom. However, I have found a few areas in my life for which repentance is not the answer. Are you curious? Keep reading!

The enemy really likes to push us over into *striving*. If he can't get us into sin, he will push us to the other extreme with a religious "blood, sweat, and tears" type of mentality. This tactic is so subtle because it really plays on our desires to please the Lord and walk uprightly. We have to be aware of this pressure tactic so that we refuse striving and remain in a place of trust and rest in the grace of God.

Grace saved us, and grace keeps us. The same grace we started with is the grace that finishes us. God initiated this thing! We can trust Him to complete it. He will finish like He started, by freeing us continually *from the inside out.*

"Then on the most important day of the feast, the last day, Jesus stood and shouted out to the crowds— "All you thirsty ones, come to me! Come to me and drink! Believe in me so that rivers of living water will burst out from within you, flowing from your *innermost being*, just like the Scripture says!"

—JOHN 7:37-38 TPT, EMPHASIS ADDED

"For if you embrace the truth, it will release true freedom into your lives."

—JOHN 8:32, TPT

You Can't Repent of a Wound: Tearing Down the Wall of Hopelessness

I think for me, this is probably the pivotal truth in my healing process. I remember when I first received ministry for inner healing, I didn't even know that I *needed* healing. I knew that I had issues. I knew that I needed to be fixed, but I didn't know that at the core of my issues were wounds.

In the natural, we know we cannot just leave a wound (especially a traumatic one) unattended. It must be cleansed. Medicines must be applied. Proper bandages must cover it for some time. A physician or experienced caregiver is often needed to examine the wound for infection to ensure that healing is progressing.

We would never even consider going about life as usual if we have a gaping, painful, debilitating injury. *Yet, this is what many Christians do!* They do not do it out of rebellion, but out of ignorance. We learn very early how to manage our pain the wrong way. We can even become highly functioning in our dysfunction, but this is not the life that our Savior died to give us. This is why Jesus came!

"A thief has only one thing in mind—he wants to steal, slaughter, and destroy. But I have come to give you everything in abundance, more than you expect —life in its fullness until you overflow!"

—JOHN 10:10, TPT

One way I think of it is living below the spiritual poverty line. Abundant life is our gift from Jesus. It is what He paid the price for. It is our inheritance from which we are meant to live.

---

*Any area of our lives in which
we are experiencing less than
abundance is an area where
He wants to set us free!*

His will for us is abundant peace, abundant joy, and abundant love. *These are the hallmarks of a life set free.* Lack or poverty in *these* areas of our soul are indicators of deeper issues that need the Great Physician's great care.

Here is where many Christians believe a lie and fall into a common trap. Because they are not experiencing freedom in a certain area, that low-level living becomes their reality. It becomes familiar, and accommodations are made to adjust to that reality. Perhaps a person deals with anxiety when he has to read aloud publicly. Some mild anxiety, of course, would be normal, but this is not normal. An extreme anxiety of not being able to read with flow at all, stuttering, sweating, and panic attacks, are not normal. He may even ask for God's help, but still no change. They try not to panic, but it is overwhelming. The cycle of repenting, praying, and trying harder is quite a rut to be in. Frankly, victory in this area seems hopeless, and it is, until the root of the fear is addressed.

We all know what it's like pulling weeds. Until the roots are destroyed, we can count on seeing the same shoots and fruits popping up over, and over, and over.

Well, looking back at this example, what is this person's root? What if in his childhood he had a harsh and overbearing parent who berated him verbally for his oral reading skills? And we're not just talking about once or twice, but they chronically berated him. These abusive actions created a wound in his soul which never healed.

I want to interject here to say that what may be traumatic to one person may not be to another. We are all unique, and we uniquely process events that happen in our lives. Surprisingly, even children in the same family may experience the same wounds but deal with them or process them differently. This is why learning to forgive quickly and freely is so powerful!

So, later in life, this person is trying so hard to be free. He's repenting again and again of this shameful anxiety, but the truth is that he cannot repent of a wound.

Wounds are meant for healing.

This was very good news to me! After many years of being a church-going, Bible-believing, God-loving Christian, I was so relieved to finally discover that Christianity was not meant to be full of striving! After years of singing and believing that old song *Victory in Jesus,* I found out that it is possible. Victory is possible!

God doesn't want me or you to ignore our wounds. He also doesn't want us to strive with them. He wants to heal them. He does not want us to be a "whack-a-mole" believer, constantly trying to deal with the results of a root trauma. He wants to heal the trauma, remove the lies attached to it, and replace it with truth in our inward parts. He doesn't want us to be ashamed of our wounds, and He also doesn't want us to treasure or coddle our wounds. He wants us whole.

You Can't Repent of Being You: Tearing down the Wall of Shame

Let's talk about this enemy of peace and victory, which is shame! Let's get busy exposing it and evicting it!

In the Church, we often lump together the terms shame, guilt, and condemnation as if they are interchangeable. However, they are quite different, and understanding the differences can be helpful. I would define shame as that nagging sense that something is intrinsically wrong with us. It is often confused with guilt, but guilt is the sense that I have sinned and should be punished. Condemnation is a legal term, it is the actual punishment for law-breaking.

All healthy humans experience guilt after wrongdoing, and if we yield, it will lead us to the cross where Jesus bore our punishment and our condemnation. As it says in Romans chapter 8, there is no longer any condemnation upon us once we receive Christ. In Christ, we are declared not guilty in the court of heaven. Our guilt was taken by Jesus upon the cross as well as our punishment. He also took for us the result of our sin, which is our bruising or inner wounds. Wow! So complete and wonderful is our salvation! What a savior, healer, and deliverer is Jesus!

> "So, what does all this mean? If God has determined to stand with us, tell me, who then could ever stand against us? For God has proved his love by giving us his greatest treasure, the gift of his Son. And since God freely offered him up as the sacrifice for us all, he certainly won't withhold from us anything else he has to give. Who then would dare to accuse those whom God has chosen in love to be his? God himself is the judge who has issued his final verdict over them—'Not guilty!' Who then is left to condemn us? Certainly not Jesus, the Anointed One! For he gave his life for us, and even more than that, he has conquered death and is now risen, exalted, and enthroned by God at his right hand. So how could he possibly condemn us since he is continually praying for our triumph?"
>
> — Romans 8:31-34, TPT

Why then do so many of us carry the weight of our sins and failures? Shame is the reason. It is a very effective tool of the enemy, and we need to be wise to it.

While guilt and condemnation are the natural results of wrong actions and lead us to the cross, shame is a different beast. It has to do, not with our actions, but with *who we are*. Shame will cause us to feel unclean, dirty, wrong, unworthy, and less-than in our identity. It is like a weight, a heavy burden, that yokes us to our pre-Christ identity. We want to see ourselves through God's eyes of grace and sonship, but shame keeps us in duality, a place of limbo, where we can't seem to reconcile who we have been in the past with who we are in Christ.

Shame says to us that we can only go so far as a Christian, and that we are somehow less than others. Shame wants you to believe that you are disqualified, and that there is something wrong with you. Shame tries to convince you that you are second-rate, adopted as God's child but without the privileges of the true sons and daughters. Oh friends, can you see why this is such a favorite weapon of our adversary?

Shame keeps us from true intimacy.

Shame will keep us always outside of true intimacy with God and man because it causes us to feel deep down that we aren't like everyone else around us. We believe that if people saw the true us, they would reject us. It is as if shame has stamped us with the word "rejected." We expect rejection, and if it doesn't come soon enough, then we force it by *tempting* others to reject us.

Angry, fearful people will often proclaim the words *shame on you* when they want to hurt those who have done wrong. Can you see how this is actually a word curse? Those are powerfully damaging words, and we should not utter them. We are of a different spirit, so we should bless and not curse.[1]

Yes, humans may try to use shame as a tool to manipulate, but Shame is *not* a tool that God uses to bring us to repentance. True repentance will in fact relieve us and free us from guilt, but it is not the remedy for shame. Why? Because you can't repent of being *you*!

Well, there's the problem! We can't be in agreement with shame and also love ourselves at the same time. God loves us dearly, and it saddens Him when we fail to value and love ourselves healthily. We must have a divine exchange. The wonderful news is that this is the exchange God delights in making!

> "To appoint unto them that mourn in Zion, to give unto them beauty for ashes, the oil of joy for mourning, the garment of praise for the spirit of heaviness; that they might be called trees of righteousness, the planting of the Lord, that he might be glorified."
>
> — Isaiah 61:3, NAS

> "Instead of your shame you will have a double portion, And instead of humiliation they will shout for joy over their portion. Therefore they will possess a double portion in their land, Everlasting joy will be theirs."
>
> — Isaiah 61:7, NAS

Ask God to show you at what point in life you shook hands with and partnered with shame. It may have come through an abuse, or maybe from being raised in poverty and neglect. It may have come through a sin you committed or a sin committed against you. It may be generational. Whatever the cause, the cure is Jesus and His blood. Forgiveness will need to be released, healing must be received, and the unholy agreement must be broken.

Finally, give God your shame. Hand to God that old familiar "friend" that has been no friend at all, and receive your divine exchange! Joy, beauty, praise, glory, worth, value, stability, and a double portion are far better accompaniments to your walk with God. Boldly and proudly wear your crown of glory, and your robe of righteousness. After all, that is who you *really* are.

You Can't Repent of a Need: Tearing Down the Wall of Condemnation

Guilt is a powerful, *powerful* force. It will not be ignored or stifled. It will drive us to *do* something. These are some of the types of things that guilt can drive you to do:

- Hide or escape from it
- Self-medicate from the pain of it
- Angrily accuse those we feel accuse us of it
- Blame shift and find a scapegoat to carry it away
- Or, Come to the cross where guilt is removed, fully

Guilt is helpful. It is the natural result of wrong actions. It is a stain upon our soul that only forgiveness can remove. It doesn't feel good. It is a crushing weight...a weight that God Himself bore on the cross so that we don't have to.

The good news is that we can exchange our guilt today for God's love and forgiveness. His message to us is one of relief.

> "Are you weary, carrying a heavy burden? Then come to me. I will refresh your life, for I am your oasis. Simply join your life with mine. Learn my ways and you'll discover that I'm gentle, humble, easy to please. You will find refreshment and rest in me. For all that I require of you will be pleasant and easy to bear."
>
> — Matthew 11:28-30, TPT

***Repentance is the remedy for guilt,
but it is not the remedy for a need.***

As we have already discussed, needs are legitimate and real. They are neither good nor bad. They just are part of the human experience called life!

So, quite simply, we must be careful not to over spiritualize our needs. If I feel lonely, I may need to call a friend. That doesn't make me weak, it makes me human! If I feel down, I may need to watch a funny movie. If I am hungry, unless I am fasting, I should eat (and it's just fine if it is yummy). If I feel tired, I should rest. If I feel drained, I may need a hug from a real person, who wears skin.

Listen, it totally delights the heart of God when He sees His children meeting each other's needs. As long as He has first place, it's all good. He *absolutely* wants your needs met.

Never stuff your needs. Acknowledge them, and give them the proper attention by meeting them in healthy ways. This pleases God. Remember, He is our Good Shepherd. He doesn't want us to want!

Summary

- I can't repent of a wound. Wounds must be healed.
- I can't repent of being me. I am perfectly loved by God just as I am, *while* I am getting whole.
- I can't repent of a need. Needs don't make me unholy; they make me human.
- Scriptures for deeper study: John 7:37-38; John 8:32; John 10:10; Isaiah 61:3-7; Matthew 11:28-30; Romans 8:31-34.

Prayer

Lord, I am sorry for any way that I have rejected myself. I know that You love me and that You like me. I know that I am Your beloved child. I ask You to forgive me, and I choose to forgive myself for _____. *(List any sin or mistake that comes up in your heart.) I receive Your forgiveness and cleansing. Lord, I confess that I have agreed with shame. Forgive me for making that agreement. In Jesus's name, I now break that agreement. I renounce the lie that I should be ashamed of myself in any way. I agree with You, Lord, that I am right (righteous), not wrong, because of Your blood and because of Your love. Now Jesus, I hand to you Shame and all of its fruit in my life. What do You want to give me instead?* (Whatever He shows you, receive it and write it down.)

Faith Declaration

"There is *nothing* wrong with me."

Activation

Meditate on this:

> Deliverance or inner-healing does not *alter* you. *It frees the real you to emerge.* You will not become super-spiritual, mystical, or mysterious. You will actually be more human, more transparent, and more real. When the real you is covered up in bondage and distorted by brokenness, you can't see who you really are, and neither can anyone else. Some people say, "What if I don't like the real me?" Believe me, you will like the real you that God created. The real you is wonderful, witty, considerate, pure, peaceful, attractive, dynamic, positive, fulfilled, and full of purpose. I guarantee that when God is finished putting the finishing touches on you, you're going to like what you see. After all, you're going to look a lot like Jesus! But don't my word for it, take God's:

"O my beloved, you are lovely. When I see you in your beauty, I see a radiant city where we will dwell as one. More pleasing than any pleasure, more delightful than any delight, you have ravished my heart, stealing away my strength to resist you. Even hosts of angels stand in awe of you. Turn your eyes from me; I can't take it anymore! I can't resist the passion of these eyes that I adore. Overpowered by a glance, my ravished heart—undone. Held captive by your love, I am truly overcome! For your undying devotion to me is the most yielded sacrifice. The shining of your spirit shows how you have taken my truth to become balanced and complete. Your beautiful blushing cheeks reveal how real your passion is for me, even hidden behind your veil of humility. I could have chosen any from among the vast multitude of royal ones who follow me. But one is my beloved dove—unrivaled in beauty, without equal, beyond compare, the perfect one, the favorite one. Others see your beauty and sing of your joy. Brides and queens chant your praise: 'How blessed is she!' Look at you now— arising as the dayspring of the dawn, fair as the shining moon. Bright and brilliant as the sun in all its strength. Astonishing to behold as a majestic army waving banners of victory."

— SONG OF SONGS 6:4-10, TPT

PART 4

UNVEILED BY GOD — The Place of Transformation

What if your destiny in God is even more than you've hoped it could be? As you shake off the dust of sin's residue and the veil of religious striving, you will rise (with Holy Spirit buoyancy) into your new life, the resurrection life of Jesus Christ.

You are not of this world any longer, and the life you now live is Jesus' own life. *You are empowered by the very life of God.* That glorious reality must be our focus—not sin, failures, frailty, or performance. In this next section, we are going to do just that! We are going to fix our gaze on Jesus, His fiery passion (which fuels us[1]), His river of life that fills us, and the beautiful secret place of intimacy where we abide with Him.

He is all we will ever need.

A POWERFUL PROMISE

Power to Trample

"Now you understand that I have imparted to you all my authority to trample over his kingdom. You will trample upon every demon before you and overcome every power Satan possesses. Absolutely nothing will be able to harm you as you walk in this authority."

— LUKE 10:19, TPT

This is a truly amazing portion of scripture. It is a promise. It seems almost too good to be true. However, our Lord is not speaking in hyperbole. In fact, He is certainly giving us words to live by and to *overcome* with.

Let's break it down a bit. First of all, serpents and scorpions are clearly a reference to satan and the demonic.

"So the great dragon was thrown down once and for all. He was the serpent, the ancient snake called the devil, and Satan, who deceives the whole earth. He was cast down into the earth and his angels along with him."

— REVELATION 12:9, TPT

Jesus says He has given His disciples power to trample on demonic forces. Trample means to tread on and crush. The word *power* used here actually means "authority." We, as Christ's obedient followers, have authority over all the power of the enemy. Does the enemy have power? Yes! However, *all* of his power is *subject to the believer's authority*. This is a truth that we need to have deep down on the inside of us, written on our hearts. We have authority over *all* the power of the enemy.

If our circumstances do not match that truth, then we speak to our circumstances. We speak to the figurative mountains before us and command them to be removed. No circumstance may dictate to us what the will of God is. We have the Word and Holy Spirit. That is where we find the truth about our circumstances and about God's will for our circumstances.

I am not talking about "name it and claim it" hyper-faith. I am talking about *authority*. We can stand against any giant. We can face down any terrifying situation. Like David declared, we too can run through a horde of advancing enemy soldiers, fearless!

> "With you as my strength I can crush an enemy horde, advancing through every stronghold that stands in front of me."

— PSALM 18:29, TPT

Just think about that. He was just one man against a troop of soldiers. Why could he boldly do that? Because he knew his God. I'm pretty sure it wasn't any fun to face a horde of enemy combatants. I personally hate confrontation and avoid it when possible. *However, there is no place for passivity and complacency in the Christian life.* We are in a battle whether we like it or not. We might as well get to liking it! We might as well become handy with a sword! We might as well decide now to be *on the offense* with the enemy. He certainly is not complacent. In fact, he is an opportunist.

> "Be well balanced and always alert, because your enemy, the devil, roams around incessantly, like a roaring lion looking for its prey to devour."
>
> — 1 Peter 5:8, TPT

Like it or not, this is our adversary. *He is seeking an opportunity to devour.* I don't know about you, but this absolutely makes me want to put my fight on. I sincerely want to make any demon in my vicinity tremble in terror when I wake up each day, and I pray accordingly. I don't just say a few light prayers and start my day, but rather, I speak destruction to all the plans of the enemy with the intent of making him regret even thinking about touching me or the ones I love. Why? BECAUSE I CAN. Because, when I take my stand in the evil day,[1] I know that the Lion of the Tribe of Judah is standing over me releasing a roar that shatters the teeth of the wicked.[2]

Even though I don't like confrontation in my natural personality, I have lived in passivity before, and I already know what that will get me, which is defeat. It isn't a question of whether or not I will make it to heaven; I know I belong to God. It is a matter of deciding how my life will go *here and now* on planet earth. So, as for me and my house, I choose victory.

I hope this stirs your heart a bit to put on your armor and get into the fray. The victory has already been accomplished on the cross, but it is our privilege and responsibility to enforce the victory of Christ's shed blood.

> "Until then he is destined to reign as King until all hostility has been subdued and placed under his feet."
>
> — 1 Corinthians 15:25, TPT

"Haven't you read in the Psalms where David himself wrote: The Lord Jehovah said to my Lord, 'Sit near me in the place of authority until I subdue all your enemies under Your feet!'"

— LUKE 20:42-43, TPT

"But when this Priest had offered the one supreme sacrifice for sin for all time he sat down on a throne at the right hand of God, waiting until all his whispering enemies are subdued and turn into his footstool. And by his one perfect sacrifice he made us perfectly holy and complete for all time!"

— HEBREWS 10:12-14, TPT

Are you ready to tread? All the power of the enemy is meant to be under His feet. How? *As His people put them there.*

Nothing Will in Any Way Harm You

Here is the larger context of this passage that we just read.

"When the seventy missionaries returned to Jesus, they were ecstatic with joy, telling him, 'Lord, even the demons obeyed us when we commanded them in your name!' Jesus replied, 'While you were ministering, I watched Satan topple until he fell suddenly from heaven like lightning to the ground. Now you understand that I have imparted to you all my authority to trample over his kingdom. You will trample upon every demon before you and overcome every power Satan possesses. Absolutely nothing will be able to harm you as you walk in this authority. However, your real source of joy isn't merely that these spirits submit to your authority, but that your names are written in the journals of heaven and that you belong to God's kingdom. This is the true source of your authority.' Then Jesus, overflowing with the Holy Spirit's anointing of joy, exclaimed, 'Father, thank you, for you are Lord Supreme over heaven and earth! You have hidden the great revelation of this authority from those who are proud, those wise in their own eyes, and you have shared it with these who humbled themselves. Yes, Father. This is what pleases your heart and the very way you've chosen to extend your kingdom: to give to those who become like trusting children. Father, you have entrusted me with all that you are and all that you have. No one fully knows the Son except the Father. And no one fully knows the Father except the Son. But the Son is able to introduce and reveal the Father to anyone he chooses"'

—Luke 10:17-22, TPT

Jesus had just sent out seventy of His followers to do kingdom exploits. There is a lot of rejoicing going on here! The disciples are "ecstatic with joy." The Father is well pleased, and Jesus has one of His most joyful moments described in the Bible.

However, many of those present at this joy-fest would later die a brutal martyr's death. How then can Jesus say that nothing will be able to harm them? This verse seemed far-fetched to me at one time. Honestly, I looked at the suffering around me and in my own life and thought I must be missing something. I was! I'd like to share with you what God has taught me from this key verse.

First of all, is it possible to walk through this life unharmed? Surely, no human has achieved that level of victory. So, let's look at Jesus's life in this regard. Jesus came as the suffering servant. He fulfilled the description in Isaiah 53 of the coming messiah. He was despised, rejected, bruised, beaten, scorned, crushed, and wounded. I am definitely not boasting to have all the revelation of this verse (Luke 10:19), but what the Lord has ministered to me is this: *Through all of Jesus's suffering, His soul was unharmed.*

The harmful effects of the actions of people around Him (even those closest to Him) could not penetrate Jesus's heart and damage Him. Nothing could harm Him. His body? Yes. His mind, will, and emotions? No.

This is our inheritance as well. So, let's discuss some practical ways that we can navigate through suffering (because we are not exempt from that) without being damaged internally and mentally.

As human beings on this planet, we will have tribulation, suffering, crises, and spiritual storms that we must pass through. Jesus said that we would.

> "And everything I've taught you is so that the peace which is in me will be in you and will give you great confidence as you rest in me. For in this unbelieving world you will experience trouble and sorrows, but you must be courageous, for I have conquered the world!"
>
> —JOHN 16:33, TPT

Jesus assures us we can have peace, courage, confidence, and joy *in the midst* of hardship. Everything doesn't have to be rainbows and butterflies in order for us to rule and reign in life on this earth.

I believe this level of victorious reigning is possible under two powerful conditions, which are *His fire and His flowing river in us.* His wrap-around, fiery presence is our shield and fortress, and the living waters flowing from our belly can't be stopped up by any evil. We will discuss these two conditions further in the next few chapters, but for now, let's simply come into *agreement* with the words of Jesus. We truly have authority over *all* the power of the enemy, and we can walk this world joyful, confident, and unharmed.

This Is How We Fight Our Battles!

The life of King David gives us a powerful example of how, as lovers of God, we can walk through the most difficult of life's challenges with great peace and perhaps even a song in our heart. Just wrap your mind around that!

The Psalms written by David unveil to us the deep, intimate, and real relationship David shared with the Lord. It was frank, so honest, and so, so sweet. He learned a great secret that we all can take hold of for ourselves.

In the secret place of God's embrace,
there is perfect rest and safety.

There, we can be naked (transparent) and unafraid.

In Psalm 3, while literally in the trial of his life, David does what we all have the ability to do as well. He tucked himself lovingly and trustingly into the heart of the Father. David confided in God.

> "Lord, I have so many enemies, so many who are against me. Listen to how they whisper their slander against me, saying "Look! He's hopeless! Even God can't save him from this!" (pause in his presence) But in the depths of my heart I truly know that you, Yahweh, have become my Shield; You take me and surround me with yourself. Your glory covers me continually. You lift high my head when I bow low in shame."
>
> — Psalms 3:1-3, TPT

Completely surrounded by his enemies (including his traitorous son), his kingdom being swiped from him in a day, and on the run, he says that he *truly knows* that he is surrounded by God and His glory like an impenetrable fortress.

Grab a hold of this truth: You are also surrounded by God's glory fortress. So, be like David! Fight, live, work, serve, and praise from that place of powerful peace, the embrace of God.

"So now I'll lie down and sleep like a baby— then I'll awake in safety, for you surround me with your glory. Even though dark powers prowl around me, I won't be afraid."

— PSALMS 3:5-6, TPT

The Weapon of Joy

I would like to say a few words here concerning *joy*. One of the main strongholds in my life used to be *heaviness*. I woke up with it, spent my day with it, and fell asleep to its companionship each night. It was so familiar to me that I didn't even know it was there. *I thought it was my personality.* It's not.

Finally, I awakened to the truth that I didn't have to be heavy, depressed, or burdened—I could *choose joy!* When I found out joy was *optional*, and that I had been opting out for most of my life, it was both good news and a source of anger (righteous anger). I was ready to take the head off of that giant!

It was during this time that Joyce Meyer actually had her television viewers accept a thirty day challenge to break long-standing issues in their lives. I thought, "Challenge accepted!" It did indeed prove to be a challenge, but, I was victorious.

This is how I won:

- I took praise and worship music with me everywhere I went, and I worshipped. I didn't care who was around; I knew I had to keep my emotions up.
- I also spoke to my soul. I took my cue from David who, in the Psalms, spoke to his soul and said, "Soul, why are you so downcast? Put your hope in God!" (Psalm 42). I added to it a phrase of my own. Whenever I felt my emotions falling, I said out loud to myself, "Up, up, up!" Sound crazy? I didn't care!
- I also smiled. Yes, I smiled even when I didn't feel like it or have a good reason to. (I have since learned that science

backs this up! When we smile, feel good hormones are automatically released throughout our body.[3] Holy Spirit is so wise.)

- In addition to all this, the Lord gave me a word of wisdom that I am thrilled to share with you. This wisdom came in the form of two shifts in my thinking:

1. He said I had His permission not to worry.

You see, I felt *obligated* to worry. I treated worrying like my job. So for me, I needed to hear the Lord to say, "It's ok. I've got this." *Hear Him say that to you as well! He is holding the universe together. He will surely hold you together.*

2. He said I could be happy "for no good reason."

I had previously spent most of my life thinking that something good had to happen *externally* in order for me to be joyful *internally*. This was the big lie that kept me in partnership with the spirit of heaviness. I treated heaviness like status quo normalcy, and I treated happiness like something higher, instead of something normal or expected.
I am thrilled to say that I no longer live by that hellish lie! I feel like every day is Christmas morning. Really. Do you know why? When I realized that I don't need a good reason to be joyful, that I can just *choose* to be joyful (for "no good reason"), and nothing or nobody can stop me, it was like a dream come true!

Let me tell you the good news: Jesus has paid the *full price* for you to be joyful. Now, because of the cross, you have the *choice to be joyful.* God can do anything, but He won't make that choice for you. Before Jesus set you free by His blood, *you had no choice.* Bondage and chains were your life, but that is your life *no longer!* You are free now to make a better choice.

Here's the deal though, only *you* can make up your mind to throw off the spirit of heaviness and put on the garment of praise. Old habits may be hard to break, but on the other side of the pain of forming new habits is something priceless: a *joyful* you.

"Let joy be your continual feast."

— 1 THESSALONIANS 5:16, TPT

Summary

- Jesus has all authority, and He has given us authority over all the power of the enemy ... all means all.
- Circumstances, worldly philosophies, and the demonic will work to intimidate us to get us to *lay down our authority*, but we are called to trample them down.
- If we choose passivity, the enemy will trample us down.
- Tribulation and trials are a part of life, but with Christ, we can navigate through them victoriously and joyfully. *This is our portion and a powerful position.*
- Scripture verses for deeper study: Luke 10:17-22; 1 Peter 5:8; Psalm 18:29; Isaiah 53:3-6; John 16:33; Psalm 3; 1 Thessalonians 5:16.

Prayer

Lord, thank You. Thank You for all that You won for me at Calvary. Forgive me for in any way that I have settled for less in my life. I repent of and renounce all agreements I have made with passivity and heaviness. I now break those powers from my life, and I say they must flee me as I submit myself to Christ. I declare my freedom and my victory by the Name and the blood of Jesus. Jesus, I choose victory, and I choose joy. Help me, Lord, at every crossroads in my day (each and every day) to make the "joy choice." Help me to not forfeit even one inch of my territory to the enemy. Help me to live with my head up, shoulders back, feet planted, and sword drawn. In Jesus's mighty name, I pray. Amen.

Faith Declaration

"I am a joyful warrior!"

Activation

- Take some time in prayer and ask the Lord to reveal any unholy agreements that you may have made. Common ones are shame, heaviness, passivity, perfectionism, rejection, self-hatred, poverty, and infirmity, to name a few.

- One at a time, repent of the agreements, break them, and command the spirits to flee.

- Ask the Lord to fill you with His Spirit and give you a clean slate.

- Because these spirits are familiar to you, ask the Lord to make you especially sensitive to habits, thought patterns, and activities linked to these spirits. Ask Him to show you the triggers that cause you to want to partner with them.

- Start *your own* thirty day challenge—I dare you! Prayerfully make a game plan similar to mine but unique to you and your situation. Now, *work the plan!* Experts say that it takes twenty to thirty days to form new habits. Expect the new!

FIRE

"Those who repent I baptize with water, but there is coming a Man after me who is more powerful than I am. In fact, I'm not even worthy enough to pick up his sandals. He will submerge you into union with the Spirit of Holiness and with a raging fire! He comes with a winnowing fork in his hands and comes to his threshing floor to sift what is worthless from what is pure. And he is ready to sweep out his threshing floor and gather his wheat into his granary, but the straw he will burn up with a fire that can't be extinguished!"

— MATTHEW 3:11-12, TPT

Many years ago I watched a video of the very fiery Reinhard Bonnke preaching in Africa. I was greatly impacted by his message, and therefore still remember it to this today, over twenty years later. It was a very simple message, titled "Keep the Fire Burning."

Hot for God

During his message, he shared a story to illustrate the importance of being *hot for God*. A Christian woman came up to him for prayer and began describing her dilemma. In a very emotional discourse, she told of how she was being tormented by a demon sitting on her head. No matter what she tried, she couldn't get the demon to leave. Reinhard said he listened and listened to her describing this demon on her head and was internally asking the Holy Spirit how to help her. This is the wisdom that God gave him. He said to her, "A fly cannot sit on a hot stove!"

Those few simple words have long stuck with me and helped me. Oh, how simple this Christian life is meant to be! *Not necessarily easy, but simple.*

Things only get complicated
when we have lost the fire.

When I am wrestling with Holy Spirit over an idol I want to hold on to, things get complicated. When I cling to unhealthy choices, things get complicated. When I rationalize my bad behavior instead of repenting, it gets complicated. So how do we keep the fire burning? Simply surrender.

First the Sacrifice Then the Fire

There is a beautiful pattern in scripture of God's fire falling on a pleasing sacrifice. Even as far back as Cain and Abel, we can see a hint of it. How do we know that Cain's offering was rejected? Most likely, he knew it had been rejected because no fire fell on his offering. The fire on the sacrificial offering was proof that God was pleased with the offering.

We see it again in the story of Elijah and the prophets of Baal. No matter what they tried, the false prophets could get no response from their god. Elijah simply made an offering and prayed and fire fell in abundance. Let's look at the story:

"Then said Elijah unto the people, I, even I only, remain a prophet of the Lord; but Baal's prophets are four hundred and fifty men. Let them therefore give us two bullocks; and let them choose one bullock for themselves, and cut it in pieces, and lay it on wood, and put no fire under: and I will dress the other bullock, and lay it on wood, and put no fire under: And call ye on the name of your gods, and I will call on the name of the Lord: and the God that answereth by fire, let him be God. And all the people answered and said, It is well spoken.

And it came to pass, when midday was past, and they prophesied until the time of the offering of the evening sacrifice, that there was neither voice, nor any to answer, nor any that regarded. And Elijah said unto all the people, Come near unto me. And all the people came near unto him. And he repaired the altar of the Lord that was broken down. And Elijah took twelve stones, according to the number of the tribes of the sons of Jacob, unto whom the word of the Lord came, saying, Israel shall be thy name: And with the stones he built an altar in the name of the Lord: and he made a trench about the altar, as great as would contain two measures of seed. And he put the wood in order, and cut the bullock in pieces, and laid him on the wood, and said, Fill four barrels with water, and pour it on the burnt sacrifice, and on the wood. And he said, Do it the second time. And they did it the second time. And he said, Do it the third time. And they did it the third time. And the water ran round about the altar; and he filled the trench also with water. And it came to pass at the time of the offering of the evening sacrifice, that Elijah the prophet came near, and said, Lord God of Abraham, Isaac, and of Israel, let it be known this day that thou art God in Israel, and that I am thy servant, and that I have done all these things at thy word. Hear me, O Lord, hear me, that this people may know that thou art the Lord God, and

that thou hast turned their heart back again. Then the fire of the
Lord fell, and consumed the burnt sacrifice, and the wood, and the
stones, and the dust, and licked up the water that was in the
trench. And when all the people saw it, they fell on their faces: and
they said, The Lord, he is the God; the Lord, he is the God."

—1 Kings 18:22-24, 29-39, KJV

Again, in the book of Acts, as the 120 followers of Jesus waited in
the upper room for the promise of the Holy Spirit, why didn't they
just have a nice little prayer meeting for a few pious hours and then
head on home? Why go on day after day after day? How did they
know that He hadn't come? No fire.

"On the day Pentecost was being fulfilled, all the disciples were
gathered in one place. Suddenly they heard the sound of a violent
blast of wind rushing into the house from out of the heavenly
realm. The roar of the wind was so overpowering it was all anyone
could bear! Then all at once a pillar of fire appeared before their
eyes. It separated into tongues of fire that engulfed each one of
them. They were all filled and equipped with the Holy Spirit and
were inspired to speak in tongues—empowered by the Spirit to
speak in languages they had never learned!"

— Acts 2:1-4, TPT

The sign was the fire. Each believer was a candle with his own flame
atop his head. This is the scriptural precedent for every New Testament believer. *We are meant to be aflame.*

Burning Ones

Another powerful illustration of this is seen in a ritual performed
year after year during the Jewish feast of tabernacles. It was the
ritual of the illumination of the temple. The feast lasted for eight
days, and every evening the priests would light four huge candle-

sticks that were seventy-five feet high! Each candlestick had four lamps. The lamps were so tall and bright that they lit up the entire temple mount all night and could be seen from a distance. It was remarkable.

Yearly, this powerfully symbolic ritual was enacted faithfully, pointing men's hearts to an unconquerable light. A light that, as it says in John chapter one, darkness cannot overcome, the Lord Jesus. And He came! The light came into the world. On one fateful morning during His earthly ministry, Jesus came into the temple courts just as these lights were being extinguished. With that amazing prophetic backdrop, He stood and proclaimed, "I Am the light to the world!" The ritual was fulfilled. The light had come! (John 8:12).

Jesus declared Himself the Light of the world, but that's not all. He also pronounced that we, His Church, are also the light of the world and the illuminated temple that can't be hidden by darkness.

> "Your lives light up the world. Let others see your light from a distance, for how can you hide a city that stands on a hilltop? And who would light a lamp and then hide it in an obscure place? Instead, it's placed where everyone in the house can benefit from its light. So don't hide your light! Let it shine brightly before others, so that the commendable things you do will shine as light upon them, and then they will give their praise to your Father in heaven."
>
> — MATTHEW 5:14-16, TPT

How does our light shine? Commendable deeds, good works. This is more than acts of kindness. It is that, certainly, but in a larger sense it is manifesting the kingdom of heaven into darkened earthly circumstances. Bringing God's rule and reign upon the earth. Bringing His love to love-starved humanity is an aspect of His dominion.

Again this was pictured in the four great candlesticks. Those great lights were a powerful prophetic illustration of the overcoming, fiery church of the living God. *We are His burning ones.* The flames were four by four: four flames atop four stands. The number four is symbolic of God's heavenly rule and order coming into the earth realm. For example, there are four seasons, four directions, four elements in nature, four living creatures, and four gospels. The fourth day of creation brought the sun, moon and stars, necessary to establish times and seasons. Jesus Himself came on the 4,000th year of creation and established a new order of divine worship. He said to the Samaritan woman at the well (John 4) that the time of worshipping at a place was over; now we worship in our hearts in spirit and truth. He fulfilled the former order of the law and prophets and brought the new law of the spirit of life. Now, we who are His burning ones are establishing His kingdom here on earth as we live and pray, "Thy Kingdom come, Thy will be done." Now, *we* bring His order and government through spirit-led lives displayed in commendable works. *We shine His light!*

Anything less than a fiery heart is less than what Christ paid for on Calvary. *We are meant for fire.* Anything less is a perversion of the pattern of the church given at Pentecost. We don't, however, need to strive for fire. No, the fire falls upon our surrendered lives, living sacrifices.

William Booth the famous founder of the Salvation Army wrote the great revival hymn *Send the Fire*. These lyrics are absolutely powerful:

Thou Christ of burning, cleansing flame,

Send the fire, send the fire, send the fire!

Thy blood bought gift today we claim,

Send the fire, send the fire, send the fire!

Look down and see this waiting host,

Give us the promised Holy Ghost;

We want another Pentecost,

Send the fire, send the fire, send the fire!

God of Elijah, hear our cry:

Send the fire, send the fire, send the fire!

To make us fit to live or die,

Send the fire, send the fire, send the fire!

To burn up every trace of sin,

To bring the light and glory in,

The revolution now begin,

Send the fire, send the fire, send the fire!

'Tis fire we want, for fire we plead,

Send the fire, send the fire, send the fire!

The fire will meet our every need,

Send the fire, send the fire, send the fire!

For strength to ever do the right,

For grace to conquer in the fight,

For power to walk the world in white,

Send the fire, send the fire, send the fire!

To make our weak hearts strong and brave,

Send the fire, send the fire, send the fire!

To live a dying world to save,

Send the fire, send the fire, send the fire!

O see us on Thy altar lay

Our lives, our all, this very day;

To crown the offering now we pray,

Send the fire, send the fire, send the fire!

Not Easy ... SIMPLE

My favorite line in the song is *Tis fire we want, for fire we plead ... the fire will meet our every need.* The older I get and the more I learn, the more I see how very simple it's meant to be. The fire will meet our every need. In other words, *the fire will put things back into divine order.* Truly, a fly can't sit on a hot stove.

The fire will put things back into divine order.

The book of James puts it this way: "So then, surrender to God. Stand up to the devil and resist him and he will turn and run away from you" (James 4:7, TPT). The requirements for fire to fall have never changed, and it may not always be easy, but it is simple. Submit, surrender, lay it all down. Be a living sacrifice. If you become a whole burnt offering, your fleshly desires will be consumed, and what is left will be wholly pleasing to God.

> "Beloved friends, what should be our proper response to God's marvelous mercies? I encourage you to surrender yourselves to God to be his sacred, living sacrifices. And live in holiness, experiencing all that delights his heart. For this becomes your genuine expression of worship."

> — ROMANS 12:1, TPT

True Worship

We also see the whole burnt offering in Genesis 22 in the account of the offering of Isaac on Mt. Moriah. Wow, what a powerful picture. This is actually the first mention of worship in the Bible.

> "He said, 'Take now your son, your only son, whom you love, Isaac, and go to the land of Moriah, and offer him there as a burnt offering on one of the mountains of which I will tell you.' So Abraham rose early in the morning and saddled his donkey, and took two of his young men with him and Isaac his son; and he split wood for the burnt offering, and arose and went to the place of which God had told him. On the third day Abraham raised his eyes and saw the place from a distance. Abraham said to his young men, 'Stay here with the donkey, and I and the lad will go over there; and we will worship and return to you.'"
>
> — Genesis 22:2-5, NASB

This was a beautiful prophetic picture of the offering of Jesus Christ on the cross for us. We see an important principle that we must embrace, which is that worship and sacrifice are *linked*. Worship is laying down our all—our lives, our best, our treasure—on the altar.

The whole burnt offering was unique. It was laid out piece by piece and completely consumed. No part was withheld. It was devoted completely to God; none of it was eaten by man. It was personal and voluntary by the offeror; it was painstakingly killed, cut up, and placed on the fire, personally. It was costly, and it beautifully depicts our life of pure love and complete devotion to God.

> "At each and every sunrise you will hear my voice as I prepare my sacrifice of prayer to you. Every morning I lay out the pieces of my life on the altar and wait for your fire to fall upon my heart."
>
> — Psalm 5:3, TPT

Peace is the atmosphere in which every Christian is meant to abide. Peace is the automatic byproduct of *right standing with God.* When our peace is disrupted, it is an indicator that something is out of kilter.

We should never ignore it when our peace is disrupted.

It is important to just take a moment and take inventory. Remember earlier, we talked about how there are only two types of warfare. Disrupted peace is either an issue of the enemy attacking us from legal ground he has in our life, *or* he is harassing us in an attempt to hinder our moving forward with God. In either case, a fly can't sit on a hot stove! *Submit, resist, and he will flee.*

Another interesting fact about those wondrous seventy-five feet tall lamps is that the wicks for the lamps were made from the used linen undergarments of the priests. The symbolism here is simply breath-taking. Why would God have them do such a thing? Why did He care what the wicks were made of? It is a powerful prophetic picture again of His burning, blazing church.

Throughout scripture, linen represents *the righteousness and righteous acts of the saints.*

> "Fine linen, shining bright and clear, has been given to her to wear, and the fine linen represents the righteous deeds of his holy believers."
>
> — REVELATION 19:8, TPT

Undergarments are symbolic of our inner life—our innermost being—that which only God fully sees and fully knows. The linen undergarments of the priests symbolize the *pure inner life of God's servant.*

What then are we to learn from this? God provides the fire. He even provides the oil (of His Spirit) for fuel. *But each of us must provide the pure hearts and lives surrendered before His eyes in sincere worship.* We don't have to be perfect. We just must be His, fully. This righteousness produces the fruit of peace we are meant for.

On a side note—looking back to the story of the dear lady with "a demon sitting on her head"—don't be surprised if the enemy acts stubbornly. There are accounts in the Bible of Jesus telling demons to be quiet, and they instead came out with a shriek. I'm not sure how to file that doctrinally, but it does teach me to stand my ground. There will be times when we will have to enforce Christ's victory with perseverance, faith, and stamina. However, the bottom line is that *if we don't quit, we win!*

We use *all* the weapons in our arsenal. If all the doors of access in our life have been shut through healing and repentance, it is time to get our praise on, our worship on, and our combat boots on. Again, if we are His submitted and living sacrifices, then the fire of God is on our life. We take our stand in the evil day and resist and keep on resisting *until the enemy flees.*

Turn Up The Heat

I had an experience in my life where God reminded me once again of the importance of the fire. I had spent a day in a spiritually yucky environment. I was with people that I loved, but who were not believers, and when I left, I just felt slimed. I rebuked the enemy and bound this and that, but I still felt like something was "on" me.

I was lying in bed later that night and was wondering what I needed to do or pray to get rid of the yuck when the Holy Spirit gently whispered, "A fly can't sit on a hot stove." I knew exactly what He was saying: It's time to turn up the heat and worship. So, I did.

In that place of greatest intimacy (where it's just you and Jesus), guess what? It's *just* you and Jesus because no demons can handle that fire. Keep the fire burning!

Kiss - Kindle - Armor

The Shulamite maiden of the Song of Songs cries out to the Shepherd King for his kiss.

> "Let him smother me with kisses—his Spirit-kiss divine. So kind are your caresses, I drink them in like the sweetest wine!"
>
> — SONG OF SONGS 1:2, TPT

What a poignant heart cry. Is it yours as well? This is a heart-level yearning for life-union with God. It came from one who was tired and worn out from religious duty in the absence of deep communion. Like the maiden of the Song, we too can never be truly satisfied with anything less than intimate connection with Jesus—His kisses.

The Hebrew word for kiss is *nashaq*. It has three meanings: kiss, kindle, and armor. A kiss requires a face to face encounter. Kindle suggests the fire and holy passion ignited in that encounter. And armor is the clothing of strength and protection that equips us as God's warrior bride. *What a beautiful message.* In His kiss, in that place of intimacy, not only are our needs for love and connection with God met, but we are also ignited by the fiery flame of His presence and armored for battle!

> "Fasten me upon your heart as a seal of fire forevermore. This living, consuming flame will seal you as my prisoner of love. My passion is stronger than the chains of death and the grave, all consuming as the very flashes of fire from the burning heart of God. Place this fierce, unrelenting fire over your entire being. Rivers of pain and persecution will never extinguish this flame. Endless floods will be unable to quench this raging fire that burns

within you. Everything will be consumed. It will stop at nothing as you yield everything to this furious fire until it won't even seem to you like a sacrifice anymore."

— Song of Songs 8:6-7, TPT

Summary

- I am meant to be a candle burning with the flame of the Lord.
- My job is to present myself as a sacrifice. God's job is to send the fire, *and He will.*
- The fire of God on my life accomplishes what nothing and no one else can: It burns away everything but me and God.
- I don't have to pray harder, work harder, or try harder to get the fire. I just have to submit to God as a living sacrifice on the altar.
- Scriptures for deeper study: 1 Kings 18:22-29, Acts 2:1-4, Matt. 5:14-16, John 8:12; James 4:7, Rom. 12:1, Psalm 5:3, Matt. 3:11-12.

Prayer

Father, set Your seal of fiery love upon my heart. I lay myself down at Your feet as a love offering. Please burn away everything that hurts or hinders my relationship with You. Consume me with Your fire until my passions are fixed on one thing—You. All I want is You. Come, Lord. Come as a consuming fire. Come any way that You wish. Thank You, Lord. Amen.

Faith Declaration

"I burn with a zealous, fiery, white-hot passion for God."

Activation

Sometimes in the busyness of life, we end up giving God the dregs of our day. Set aside some time that you know you won't have to cut off at a certain point. Give the Lord some unlimited time. Have no agenda other than to simply be with Him, worship at His feet, and wait upon Him. Give Him your "kisses," your love words, and receive His sweet love words as well. Abide in that face to face communion and be kindled with fresh passion and fire. Become His burning one.

18

HIS FLOWING RIVER

"Pay attention to the welfare of your innermost being, for from there flows the wellspring of life."

— PROVERBS 4:23B, TPT

*W*e have discussed one way in which we can be safe from harm—being too hot for the enemy to handle. Another key to being safeguarded from spiritual harm is having a continual life flow of the Holy Spirit pouring out of us.

Then on the most important day of the feast, the last day, Jesus stood and shouted out to the crowds— 'All you thirsty ones, come to me! Come to me and drink! Believe in me so that rivers of living water will burst out from within you, flowing from your innermost being, just like the Scripture says!'"

— JOHN 7:37-38, TPT

Fullness

The last portion of that verse from John 7 can also be translated as *rivers of living water will flow from his throne within.*[1] Friends, this is the river of life of Revelation 22 and Ezekiel 47. *It flows within us!*

Sadly, even though I was raised in church, this was not the model of Christianity I was taught to expect and to live. Sure, we had special revival meetings, services, and retreats, and I so thank God for how He graciously moved and touched my heart in those times, but that is not *fullness*. We are meant for fullness.

> ### *Jesus paid the price, with His own blood, for your fullness.*

If we are not living in the fullness of His Spirit, then we are living below what Jesus purchased for us on Calvary, *and* we are susceptible to spiritual harm. So, let's talk more about this fullness!

> "And now out of his fullness we are fulfilled! And from him we receive grace heaped upon more grace!"
>
> —JOHN 1:16, TPT

> "Jesus was prophesying about the Holy Spirit that believers were being prepared to receive. But the Holy Spirit had not yet been poured out upon them, because Jesus had not yet been unveiled in his full splendor."
>
> —JOHN 7:39, TPT

As John the Baptist preached and prepared the way in people's hearts for Jesus and for the outpouring of the Spirit, he said this:

"The real action comes next: The star in this drama, to whom I'm a mere stagehand, will change your life. I'm baptizing you here in the river, turning your old life in for a kingdom life. His baptism— a holy baptism by the Holy Spirit—will change you from the inside out."

— Mark 1:7-8, MSG

"Those who repent I baptize with water, but there is coming a Man after me who is more powerful than I am. In fact, I'm not even worthy enough to pick up his sandals. He will submerge you into union with the Spirit of Holiness and with a raging fire!"

— Matthew 3:11, TPT

We can see in these verses that we were never meant to accomplish *anything* by our own strength, ability, or might. We are meant for a dynamic relationship with the living God through the Holy Spirit, who changes us from the inside out. This baptism is a complete immersion in Him. *It is what makes the kingdom life all it should be.*

The word "baptism" comes from the Greek word *baptizo.*

Baptizo[2]:

- to dip repeatedly, to immerse, to submerge (of vessels sunk)
- to cleanse by dipping or submerging, to wash, to make clean with water, to wash one's self, bathe
- to overwhelm
- (Not to be confused with bapto[3])

In studying it, I found this very good description of baptism that paints a great picture for a model of the Christian walk:

The clearest example that shows the meaning of baptizo is a text from the Greek poet and physician Nicander, who lived about 200 B.C. It is a recipe for making pickles and is helpful because it uses both words. Nicander says that in order to make a pickle, the vegetable should first be 'dipped' (bapto) into boiling water and then 'baptised' (baptizo) in the vinegar solution. Both verbs concern the immersing of vegetables in a solution. But the first is temporary. The second, the act of baptizing the vegetable, produces a permanent change. When used in the New Testament, this word more often refers to our union and identification with Christ than to our water baptism.[4]

Our life is to be lived in *union* with Jesus. In that place of union, we are permanently changed. It is not a mere dip occasionally, but repeatedly. We need a *continual* fullness of Him. The words: immerse, submerge, cleanse by dipping, wash, make clean, bathe, and to overwhelm are clearly the results of a ***flowing river***, not a wading pool.

Living in The Flow

"Believe in me so that rivers of living water will burst out from within you, flowing from your innermost being."

—JOHN 7:38, TPT

BELIEVE: Life Union Brings the Life Flow

Salvation and regeneration must be by faith. True faith (*pistis* in the Greek) has a number of components. It means acceptance, embracing something as truth, confidence that God alone is enough, and it also means *union with God and his Word*. This is so important! Believing brings us into union with God which releases the life flow of His spirit in us.

RIVERS: Flood, River, Stream, Water,

to Drink, Drinkable, Banqueting

Interestingly, this word for rivers in the Greek only occurs three times in scripture. Two of those times, it directly references a *flood*, figuratively equivalent to the greatest of abundance. What is the message to you and I? This is not a gently trickling stream. Oh no, this is a mighty rushing river, sweeping through us and overflowing us. This is indeed *fullness*.

FLOWING: Moving Out Steadily and Continuously
in a Current or Stream in One Direction

This word is used only once in scripture, here in John 7:38. It is a description of the characteristic of waves. Scientifically, all energy flows in waves—light, sound, etc.

Here is a definition of waves from the physicsclassroom.com: "Waves involve the transport of energy without the transport of matter. In conclusion, a wave can be described as a disturbance that travels through a medium, transporting energy from one location (its source) to another location without transporting matter."[5]

God's power (Greek, *energeo*) flows through us the same way! He is the source and we are His vessel or medium. His spirit flows out from our innermost being where He dwells enthroned and touches the world around us with radiating waves of His powerful love and presence. *You and I are literally His conduits of love.*

That is so inspiring. We certainly don't want there to be anything stopping up that flow, do we? So, what actually does break waves and stop the flow? In the physical world, waves will go on forever *unless there is a disturbance.* Shallow water causes water waves to break, and friction hinders the flow of energy waves. As long as there is depth (fullness), there is a continual flow. I'm sure you can see that in the spiritual world, it is the same!

So, let's do our part and stay connected to the source so that we abide in fullness, not shallowness. Let's also avoid unnecessary friction in the riverbanks and riverbeds of our soul. Does Holy Spirit have a free and clear path to flow through and in you, or are there some blockages to freedom that need to be moved out of the way? Perhaps there are some bitter roots growing along your riverbed that God wants to uproot. Let's be quick to forgive and quick to repent when the light of God's conviction shines in our heart, so that we can be a free and powerful conduits of God's Spirit.

Free and Clear

If we come to Jesus and drink deeply, if we live from this place of fullness, if the Holy Spirit is flowing out of our life as a *river* ... how can anything unclean, toxic, or harmful enter in? It can't! Picture a water hose. If it helps, picture a firefighter's fire hose! When the faucet is turned on and the water is *flowing*, is it even possible for something to get into the mouth of that hose? No way. I believe this is how we are meant to live free and clear of the enemy's slime attacks.

How this looks in my life is that when I am starting to feel overly sensitive, irritable, too easily offended, or even slightly depressed, I need to go get a *drink* of *living water*! Truly, I need to stay right there under His precious waterfall *until I am full*.

Fullness is God's plan for us!

"And don't get drunk with wine, which is rebellion; instead be filled with the fullness of the Holy Spirit."

— EPHESIANS 5:18, TPT

"Don't drink too much wine. That cheapens your life. Drink the Spirit of God, huge draughts of him. Sing hymns instead of drinking songs! Sing songs from your heart to Christ. Sing praises over everything, any excuse for a song to God the Father in the name of our Master, Jesus Christ."

— EPHESIANS 5:18-20, MSG

"I have gathered from your heart, my equal, my bride, I have gathered from my garden all my sacred spices—even my myrrh. I have tasted and enjoyed my wine within you. I have tasted with pleasure my pure milk, my honeycomb, which you yield to me. I delight in gathering my sacred spice, all the fruits of my life I have gathered from within you, my paradise garden. Come, all my friends— feast upon my bride, all you revelers of my palace. Feast on her, my lovers! **Drink and drink, and drink again, until you can take no more.** Drink the wine of her love. Take all you desire, you priests. My life within her will become your feast."

— SONG OF SONGS 5:1, TPT, EMPHASIS ADDED

Yes, let's drink deeply.

Summary

- I am an impenetrable fortress to the fiery darts of the enemy when I am full and overflowing with the Spirit of God.
- God is a *river of cleansing* in my life. He can keep me free, pure, and peaceful.
- I must choose to be filled with the Holy Spirit. I can do my part by drinking deeply through worship, prayer, and Bible study.
- Singing songs, hymns, and spiritual songs is a key to unlock the waterfall of God's presence in my life.
- Scriptures for deeper study: John 7:37-38; Revelation 22:1; Isaiah 44:3; Ephesians 5:18-19; Mark 1:7-8; and John 1:16.

Prayer:

Father, I want fullness. I want the fullness of Your very presence in my life. Fill me, and keep on filling me, I pray. Thank You for the artesian wellspring of Your love, power, grace, joy, and wisdom overflowing in my life. Thank You that it is not by might, nor by power, but by My Spirit says the Lord (Zechariah 4:6). Hallelujah!

Faith Declaration:

"I hunger and thirst for righteousness, and I shall be filled!"

Activation:

If you don't already do this, form a new habit of daily asking God for a fresh baptism of the Spirit. This is a request which He loves to give—*"Ask and receive that your joy may be full"* (John 16:34, NIV).

FACE TO FACE IN THE SECRET PLACE

The Secret Place Of Intimacy

he secret place is the place of transformation. We have talked about a baptism of fire that consumes our lives and a baptism in the Holy Spirit that floods and overflows our spirit, but obviously there is no literal altar we climb upon and no literal fountain we drink from. So, where do we get set aflame and experience His fullness? It happens in the secret place of intimacy with Him.

There are many names for the secret place. Here is a sampling:

- The Garden of Eden (or delight) (Genesis 2)
- The cleft of the rock (Exodus 33:22)
- My Hiding place (Psalm 27:5)
- The King's chamber (Psalm 45:13)
- Your room in the father's house (John 14)
- Prayer closet (Matthew 6:6)
- Under the Shadow of Shaddai (Psalm 91)
- The heart of God (Proverbs 18:10)
- The embrace of God (Psalm 91:4)

- The king's cloud filled chamber (Song of Solomon 1:4)
- The secret stairway of the sky (Song of Solomon 2:14)
- Life-union (John 15)

Jesus paid a dear price to bring us into this place of intimacy and transformation. In fact, He left the splendor of heaven and the embrace of the trinity in order to bring us in. This is beautifully described in John chapter one.

> "In the very beginning the Living Expression was already there. And the Living Expression was with God, yet fully God. They were together— face-to-face, in the very beginning.
>
> He entered into the very world he created, yet the world was unaware. He came to the very people he created— to those who should have recognized him, but they did not receive him. But those who embraced him and took hold of his name were given authority to become the children of God!
>
> No one has ever gazed upon the fullness of God's splendor except the uniquely beloved Son, who is cherished by the Father and held close to his heart. Now he has unfolded to us the full explanation of who God truly is!"
>
> —JOHN 1:1-2, 10-12, 18, TPT

Later in John chapter 14 He describes how the invitation has been given and the way opened for the communion with God for which we long.

> "My Father's house has many dwelling places. If it were otherwise, I would tell you plainly, because I go to prepare a place for you to rest. And when everything is ready, I will come back and take you to myself so that you will be where I am. And you already know the way to the place where I'm going. ...

Jesus replied, 'Loving me empowers you to obey my word. And my Father will love you so deeply that we will come to you and make you our dwelling place.'"

—John 14:2-4, 23, TPT

Jesus and Father existed in face-to-face intimacy and created you and I for that same intimacy! Sin got in the way in the garden, but Jesus came and forever remedied the problem that sin created. The cross reconciled us fully to this place of intimacy, once and for all.

According to the footnotes in The Passion Translation, the Greek word used for "face-to-face" in John 1 (as well as the Hebraic concept conveyed) is that of being before God's face. There is no Hebrew word for presence (e.g. the presence of God), only the word *face*. Isn't that beautiful! God wants us so close. He wants us close enough to touch, to heal, to feel, to hold, to make His face to shine upon us![1]

We Are Wanted in the Secret Place

Have you ever thought about the fact that God makes special allowances and adjustments in order to be able to interact with us and be close to us? He actually *accommodates* us. He is just that beautiful and loving. He actually *wants* to be with us that *much!*

This is what I mean. If I want to interact with a toddler, I won't expect them to come up to my level. I will take off my shoes and get down on the floor and play with them on their level. Similarly, in order to keep the doors of communication open between myself and my teen children, I will have conversations with them on topics that may be unimportant to me but are desperately important to them. In order to be intimate with a grandparent and meet their need for fellowship and conversation, I won't expect them to find a way to get to me or wait for them to do something with me that I enjoy but will be too taxing for them physically. No, I will go to them! I will sit with them near their comfy recliner, with their favorite oldie but goodie playing on the TV, and talk about the news, the weather, the latest obituaries, and their aches and pains. Love makes us do those things! We make accommodations for the ones we love, and *God is no different.*

God makes sweet, kind, and loving accommodations in order to be close to us. Wow. No doubt, there are innumerable, unnoticed things He does day and night, but there are some examples I have noticed in scripture. Think about the Garden of Eden. When did God meet with Adam and Eve? He met with them and walked with them *in the cool of the evening.* Why would He do that? Was it more pleasant for God or for Adam? Listen, this isn't big, life or death theology, but it is noticeable and remarkable. He chose a time of day to come and fellowship with His children when it would be especially nice for *them.* That's just sweet.

A Cleft In The Rock

Another Bible passage in which I see this is in God's interaction with Moses in Exodus 33. This is an incredibly intimate exchange. Moses makes a request of God, "Show me Your glory." This was actually physically impossible for Moses. So God made an *accommodation.* Do you remember the story? *God provided a place for Moses,* a cleft in the rock, and put Moses there before causing all of His Glory to pass in front of Moses. As He passed His friend, God covered him with His hand as a shield, and then removed it once He passed so that Moses saw His back.

There is so much revealed in that story about God's heart toward us. Listen, there is a place for you! *Jesus is that place.* He is the rock, and we are hidden in Him. Jesus came to us, *because we could never, ever get to Him.* He accommodated us by becoming our sin and giving us His righteousness. We are so wanted by God.

Another example is the many names of God revealed in scripture. El Shaddai, Jehovah Jireh, Jehovah Rohi, Jehovah Shalom, Jehovah Shamah, etc. Most of these names were revelations to a *person through their intimate relationship with God.* Don't be offended, but there are even times in scripture where people named God. Yes, that happened. Why? Because God wants to be known by His children! He wants to know and be known, and He makes accommodations in order to *be found by us!*

> "When you come looking for me, you'll find me. Yes, when you get serious about finding me and want it more than anything else, I'll make sure you won't be disappointed..."
>
> —Jeremiah 29:13, MSG

Think for a moment of your own encounters with God. Think about your salvation experience. Did you find God, or did He let Himself be found by You? Didn't He actually set you up? Of course He did! He was working supernaturally behind the scenes, moving people and changing circumstances to get you to the right place, at the right time, in the right frame of mind. He did all of that just so that He could lay hold of your heart! He is so good at divine set ups, isn't He? That's just one of the many ways He accommodates us, by wooing us into His heart. Jesus said it this way, "You didn't choose me, but I chose you."[2] Aren't you so glad He did?

The Maker of all is after your heart! Just as He was with Moses, He will be with you, for you, too, are His beloved friend. He has special love encounters set aside *just for you*. He has presents from heaven with your name on them, waiting for you to unwrap. Don't you think He is probably like a dad on Christmas morning waiting for His child to see what He has gotten for them? I do. I think that His plans and presents for you are *unimaginable*.

> "This is why the Scriptures say: Things never discovered or heard of before, things beyond our ability to imagine— these are the many things God has in store for all his lovers. But God now unveils these profound realities to us by the Spirit. Yes, he has revealed to us his inmost heart and deepest mysteries through the Holy Spirit, who constantly explores all things. After all, who can really see into a person's heart and know his hidden impulses

except for that person's spirit? So it is with God. His thoughts and secrets are only fully understood by his Spirit, the Spirit of God."

— 1 CORINTHIANS 2:9-11, TPT

His thoughts and secrets are only fully known by His Spirit, and so He put His Spirit in us so that we could *know Him in the secret place.* In other words, He accommodates us.

God doesn't bleed. However, blood had to be shed for you and I to be redeemed. And so, God became a man in order that sacred blood could be spilled for the sins of humanity. What love!

We all at times, in one way or another, have put God into a box. We put Him in a box of our own limited understanding. And yet, He still meets us there, doesn't He? He meets us even in our brokenness, in our finiteness, in our weakness, and in our immaturity. He doesn't ever lower His standards—He can't be something He's not; He's a holy, righteous God—but, wonder of all wonders, He does indeed lower *Himself.* He bends low (accommodating our lowly humanity) in order to lift us up! This shows us three important truths about God's secret place embrace:

- We are wanted there, and He makes room for us.

- We are safe there, from accusation and from penalties.

- We are accepted there, even with our imperfections.

There Is A Place For You!

Here are a few more scriptures that describe this special place:

"Draw me into your heart. We will run away together into the king's cloud-filled chamber. We will remember your love, rejoicing and delighting in you, celebrating your every kiss as better than wine. No wonder righteousness adores you!" (Song of Songs 1:4, TPT).

"For you are my dove, hidden in the split-open rock. It was I who took you and hid you up high in the secret stairway of the sky. Let me see your radiant face and hear your sweet voice. How beautiful your eyes of worship and lovely your voice in prayer" (Song of Songs 2:14, TPT).

"So hide all your beloved ones in the sheltered, secret place before your face. Overshadow them by your glory-presence. Keep them from these accusations, the brutal insults of evil men. Tuck them safely away in the tabernacle where you dwell" (Psalms 31:20, TPT).

"There's a private place reserved for the lovers of God, where they sit near him and receive the revelation-secrets of his promises" (Psalms 25:14, TPT).

"Behold, thou art fair, my beloved, yea, pleasant: also our bed is green" (Song of Solomon 1:16, KJV).

"My beloved one, both handsome and winsome, you are pleasing beyond words. Our resting place is anointed and flourishing, like a green forest meadow bathed in light" (Song of Songs 1:16, TPT).

Our Bed (Resting Place) Is Green

Some translations of Song of Songs 1:16 say, "Our bed is verdant." The idea conveyed is that it is a place green with rich vegetation and growth. The symbolism is also rich! Our place of intimacy with the Lord is where life is found. *Life springs from that place.* Spiritual truths are conceived in that place. Dying things come alive in that place. Hope is renewed in that place.

All that we need is there, in the Secret Place,
where we are ignited and fulfilled.

The fear of the Lord is also activated through this intimacy with Him. Why? Because we are with Him there one on one, with nothing and no one else. There is no veil of separation either, nothing is hidden from His view.

If we live in that place continually (being with Him, gazing into His eyes of fire) we will want to choose the things that please Him. Knowing He is present and living like He is present changes the way we act, talk, think, and choose. If we don't live this way, it is actually practical atheism or living like God is *not present*.

Psalms 14 and 53 contain warnings against practical atheism (knowing God is real yet living and acting as if He is not). These verses teach us that a fool says in his heart there is no god. In other words, the fool thinks there is no consequence for his sinful choices. He thinks he can ignore God's ways and commands as it fits his personal wants. If we are truly honest, we will admit there are times when we have been guilty of this as well. Therefore, in order to avoid this foolish path, we *must choose to live as if God is before us always.* That reality keeps us pure.

When we live like that, worship can never be a mere act. It is a *life-style* of living honestly, humbly, and lovingly before a living God. He seeks worshippers who worship in spirit and truth. No veils, no lies, no rituals, no formulaic styles or activities—just reality with Him. In that intimate reality, where we are listening and obeying, not out of fearful dread but out of love, true holiness comes forth.

Coram Deo

Coram deo is a Latin phrase meaning "in the presence of God."[3] It summarizes the idea of Christians living in the presence of, under the authority of, and to the honor and glory of God. This is the essence of the Christian life.

To live *coram deo* is to live one's entire life before the face of God, under the authority of God, and to the glory of God. It is a delightful, thrilling, awe-inspiring, beautiful, Biblical vision of our adventure with God called life!

Do we live out our Christianity at the lowest common denominator of lukewarm love and passionless service? Do we tolerate mere status quo, mediocre affection, faith, and acts? Do we settle for "some-ness" instead of fullness? Or, do we choose to live *coram deo*! How utterly amazing that we have that choice! We can choose His face and make Him alone our passion and pleasure.

Face to Face

Life is a dance meant to be lived face to face with God. Anything less than this is less than He intended when He planted the garden and put man there. Just like with Adam and Eve, He awaits each of us to come walk and talk with Him in the cool of the day, in the sweet, refreshing breeze of His Spirit. We can be where it's God alone and find that He is *more than enough*. In that beautiful place, the sincere confession, "It's just You, God," can be said in spirit and truth.

Summary

- The secret place of intimacy with God is the place of transformation.
- It is the will, desire, and plan of God that we abide in that place, not visit.
- There, face to face—unveiled—we are fulfilled and fruitful.

- There, we truly experience the healthy fear of God that keeps us holy.
- There, we worship in spirit and in truth.
- Scriptures for deeper reading: John 1:1,2; John 14; Psalm 91; Exodus 33:12-23; Song of Solomon 1:4, 1:16, 2:14; and Psalm 45.

Faith Declaration

"I am wanted and welcome in the loving embrace of God. It is where I belong!"

Activation

- Spend some time picturing yourself in the garden with the Lord. Hear His words for you, and give Him your words as well. (Remember, He loves to hear your voice.) Let Him show you what He will while He pours His love into you, captivating your heart afresh.

- Prayerfully commit to having daily, face to face, alone encounters with God. Remember His promise that when you seek Him, you will find Him. He has special love encounters set aside *just for you*. He has presents with your name on them, waiting for you to unwrap.

Prayer

Lord, reignite my passion so that I will walk in a new way of grace...where my obedience flows simply from my love for You, and compassion for others is the consequence, and where I am truly living before the face of God— before Your beautiful face. Set my heart aflame with zealous love for You. Set Your seal of fiery love upon my heart. Lord, let Your holy jealousy consume me, for I confess that I am Yours and Yours alone. Amen.

PART 5

UNVEILED BY GOD — The Purpose of Transformation

God's amazing grace is taking you somewhere, and that "somewhere" is not only Heaven—it is Heaven on earth. The grace and love of God is working in you powerfully and faithfully *right now* to take you to Glory. Glory is your destiny!

Glory is simply God's goodness, Christlikeness, *Love.* God is love, so what is the goal and purpose of this journey we are all on? Simply becoming more like and more intimate with Jesus.

In this last section, let's get the big picture. The dream of God's heart is you...looking a whole lot like Jesus. And rest assured, His grace is taking you into that glorious unveiling, moment by steadfast moment, touch by gentle touch, whisper by loving whisper.

20

YOUR UNVEILING IS AT HAND

"The word of the Lord came to me, saying, 'Before I formed you in the womb I knew you, before you were born I set you apart...'"

— Jeremiah 1:4-5a, NIV

"You formed my innermost being, shaping my delicate inside and my intricate outside, and wove them all together in my mother's womb. ... You saw who you created me to be before I became me!"

— Psalms 139:13-16, TPT

You and I are each a dream birthed in the heart of God. Before you were conceived in your mother's womb, you were in God's thoughts. He imagined you...then He formed you, and now He delights in you! You are an intentional creation of God Himself, His design, His masterpiece.

Perhaps life has been unkind at times for you, and perhaps you have been bruised or marred in the dark valleys that seemed to last so long. Even so, the Lord has never changed His mind about you.

People have failed you here and there, but He never has and He never will because you are His treasure! He is in the beautiful process of restoring the beauty of who you really are, and your unveiling is glorious.

We Hope For Glory

Ours is an increasing and unfolding splendor! Our sights are on our King, and His kingdom is *glorious*. We have an ever-increasing glory:

> "We can all draw close to him with the veil removed from our faces. And with no veil we all become like mirrors who brightly reflect the glory of the Lord Jesus. We are being transfigured into his very image as we move from one brighter level of glory to another. And this glorious transfiguration comes from the Lord, who is the Spirit."
>
> — 2 CORINTHIANS 3:18, TPT

The Creation account in the Bible is an epic story of unfolding glory. Genesis reveals God's unfolding and increasing work. Here are just a few examples:

Evening to morning
Seed to plant to harvest
Bud to blossoming flower to fruit
Adam to Eve to all mankind[1]

Every aspect of His creative work reveals His long-term plan to unveil His glory. He is One who sees the end form the beginning. Before He ever said, "Let there be light" in Genesis, He was looking forward to the marriage supper of the Lamb in Revelation. You are the crown of His creation, and He is also taking you from glory to glory to glory. In fact, His grace is at work *powerfully* in you right now, not to get you to Heaven, but to get Heaven in you and through you to the world. Grace is taking you to *glory*. That is your destiny. You have a space in His divine timeline—can you picture it? In His unfolding plan, You are a part of creation's unfolding and increasing splendor:

> "I am convinced that any suffering we endure is less than nothing compared to the magnitude of glory that is about to be unveiled within us."
>
> — ROMANS 8:18, TPT

> "Living within you is the Christ who floods you with the expectation of glory! This mystery of Christ, embedded within us, becomes a heavenly treasure chest of hope filled with the riches of glory for his people, and God wants everyone to know it!"
>
> — COLOSSIANS 1:27, TPT

What is glory? It is God's goodness. It is Christ-likeness. This is our hope. This is our expectation. Therefore, a glory mindset, an expectation of being more and more like Jesus, is so important.

The Expectation of Glory

As the masterpiece of creation, mankind's "blossoming" into the glorious sons and daughters of God is the culmination all creation is yearning for. Just as the seed eventually yields its harvest, just as evening gives way to the beautiful unclouded dawn, just as the hard and earthy bud slowly and magnificently unfolds and yields its inner glory, so are you, and all creation is groaning to see that unveiling:

> "The entire universe is standing on tiptoe, yearning to see the unveiling of God's glorious sons and daughters!"
>
> — ROMANS 8:19, TPT

YOU ARE BEING UNVEILED, AND YOU ARE GOING TO BE JUST LIKE JESUS:

> "Beloved, we are God's children right now; however, it is not yet apparent what we will become. But we do know that when it is finally made visible, we will be just like him, for we will see him as he truly is."

> — 1 JOHN 3:2, TPT

YOU ARE BECOMING JESUS' LOOKALIKE PARTNER, HIS EQUAL, HIS BRIDE:

> "For you reach into my heart. With one flash of your eyes I am undone by your love, my beloved, my equal, my bride. You leave me breathless—

> I am overcome by merely a glance from your worshiping eyes, for you have stolen my heart. I am held hostage by your love and by the graces of righteousness shining upon you." Song of Songs 4:9, TPT

YOU ARE JESUS' INCREASE IN THE EARTH. Just as Eve was Adam's increase, we are Jesus' increase

> "He is the Bridegroom, and the bride belongs to him. I am the friend of the Bridegroom who stands nearby and listens with great joy to the Bridegroom's voice. And because of his words my joy is complete and overflows! So it's necessary for him to increase and for me to be diminished."

> — JOHN 3:29:30, TPT

YOU WILL RISE UP AND SHINE WITH HIS GLORY:

> "Rise up in splendor and be radiant, for your light has dawned, and Yahweh's glory now streams from you! Look carefully!

Darkness blankets the earth, and thick gloom covers the nations, but Yahweh arises upon you and the brightness of his glory appears over you!

Nations will be attracted to your radiant light and kings to the sunrise-glory of your new day. ..."

— Isaiah 60:1-2, TPT

It's Time

Beloved of God, it is time to receive your unveiling! The world will be drawn to the brightness of His shining splendor through you. Throw off every weight of sin, every yoke of fear, all the dust of your former shame, and the false covering of the veil of religion with its pressure to perform for God's love and approval. Be who you really are—"Yahweh's glory now streams from you!"

21

FREEDOM TO FOCUS

*W*e have been through quite a journey together! I pray that you have been blessed and encouraged. As you went through this book you recorded many words and pictures in the prayer activations that were a part of your own unique process of healing and freedom.

I encourage you to go back through and reread the chapter summaries, prayers, declarations, and activations, especially those things God spoke intimately and personally to you. This will help in maintaining your freedom and in forming new thought patterns and habits. Remember, God is thinking high and holy thoughts about you, so think higher thoughts along with Him!

With that in mind, I want to talk about one last thing before we end our time together. Let's talk about *focus*.

> "We can all draw close to him with the veil removed from our faces. And with no veil we all become like mirrors who brightly reflect the glory of the Lord Jesus. We are being transfigured into his very image as we move from one brighter level of glory to

another. And this glorious transfiguration comes from the Lord, who is the Spirit."

— 2 Corinthians 3:18, TPT

You were born in the natural to your parents, but you have been reborn. You have been born again, born from above. God birthed you from His heart (Deuteronomy 32:18). One of the lesser known names of God is *El Chuwl*, and it means the One Who gave you life, Who birthed you. *Chuwl* means to dance, writhe (in pains of childbirth), to birth, to bring forth (as in poetry).

You are His masterpiece!
You are His workmanship,
His poetry, the very song of His love,
birthed from His heart!

"We have become his poetry, a re-created people that will fulfill the destiny he has given each of us, for we are joined to Jesus, the Anointed One. Even before we were born, God planned in advance our destiny and the good works we would do to fulfill it!"

— Ephesians 2:10, TPT

"How beautiful on the mountains are the sandaled feet of this one bringing such good news. You are truly royalty! The way you walk so gracefully in my ways displays such dignity. You are truly the poetry of God—his very handiwork."

— Song of Songs 7:1, TPT

He is El Chuwl—He birthed us! He made us and will not abandon us. He will never forsake the one He has birthed. We are HIS. Others may fail us, but not Him.

> "Sing for joy, O heavens! Rejoice, O earth! Burst into song, O mountains! For the Lord has comforted his people and will have compassion on them in their suffering. Yet Jerusalem says, 'The Lord has deserted us; the Lord has forgotten us.' 'Never! Can a mother forget her nursing child? Can she feel no love for the child she has borne? But even if that were possible, I would not forget you! See, I have written your name on the palms of my hands. Always in my mind is a picture of Jerusalem's walls in ruins.'"
>
> — Isaiah 49:13-16, NLT

The Apple Of His Eye

God calls us the apple of His eye. This is a beautiful way of saying, "You are the center of My focus." Never doubt it. Many voices will come and scream at you trying to discredit this truth, but don't listen. Your failures, enemies, demonic spirits, and even your own heart may condemn and accuse, but hear His sweet, love words over you, "You are my beloved child. With you I am well-pleased. You are the apple of My eye."

> "He found him in a desert land, And in the howling waste of a wilderness; He encircled him, He cared for him, He guarded him as the pupil of His eye."
>
> — Deuteronomy 32:10, NASB

> "Keep me as the apple of the eye; Hide me in the shadow of Your wings."
>
> — Psalms 17:8, NASB

"Keep my commandments and live, And my teaching as the apple of your eye... they will keep you."

— PROVERBS 7:2, NASB

Over and over, in these scriptures, the concepts of keep, protection, surround, and shelter are conveyed. This is God's heart for you and me. He keeps, protect, surrounds, and shelters us with a ferocity that amazes. We are so very *loved*.

The phrase *apple of my eye* is unique to scripture. Even though it has become a somewhat common turn of phrase, it originated in God, specifically in His love for His children.

The apple of the eye is a metaphor for the pupil, the tiny opening that allows light, and therefore images, to be captured in the mind. Let's meditate on the symbolism and ideas this conveys to us. Just as the pupil is encircled and protected, so are you. Just as the pupil is the entrance into the imagination or "mind's eye," you are as the entrance to God's heart. The pupil is a gate and you have the key to God's heart!

The phrase can also be translated as daughter. In the family unit, the most protected, most precious, covered, and shielded member is the daughter. She is the "hidden treasure" within the family who, traditionally in many cultures, is given a "coming out" celebration. You are God's own hidden treasure.[1]

You are God's own hidden treasure.

It can also be translated *little man of the eye*. This meaning comes from the reflection of yourself that you see when you are face to face with someone, looking into their eyes. Listen, you are the little one in God's eye because you have been brought face to face with

Him through Christ! Now, even right at this very moment, you are reflected in His eyes. This beautiful, unique phrase *apple of my eye*, reveals that you are the center of God's focus.

Centuries ago, when the early church fathers were trying to describe the spiritual reality of the trinity, they decided to call it *perichoresis*. This word basically describes a loving, continual, union and communion in motion: a *dance!* Each member of the trinity exists face to face, in a perfect, harmonious, moving embrace. *This is what Christ's blood has brought you into.* This is your inheritance and where the change you long for happens. Indeed, He hugs us into holiness within the *perichoresis!*

You are free to now make Him, more and more each day, the center of your focus as well. He wants you eye to eye, face to face, heart to heart, and with no veils. Remember, it's a dance!

EPILOGUE

From My Heart

*I*n these closing words, I would like to share something from my own journey to freedom that has been a continuously resonating word of hope to my soul. Several years ago, when I was a young mom in my twenties, I loved the Lord so very much, and yet was so very broken. I knew the Word and was faithful in my love and service, but my glaring issues of fear, rejection, heaviness, and insecurity screamed so loudly. I knew what needed to change, but I did not know how to change. I felt hopeless in regards to real transformation and freedom.

One day while I was in prayer, I had an encounter with the Lord, and He spoke something to my heart that birthed a hope in me that I could really be free.

He spoke to me that there was a place for me in Him, and that this place was similar to when He placed Moses in the cleft of the Rock and showed him His glory. He put His hand over Moses there, and

Moses was completely hidden, covered, and safe. He was in a place of great intimacy, alone with God. It was his chrysalis.

I'm sure that Moses was never the same after that encounter. In the same way, we too are being changed from glory to glory as we abide in the secret place of His heart, our own safe chrysalis.

God revealed to me that I was in that very special, secret place and that no matter how long it might take, I was okay. I would be free to soar, and *I would see all my Egyptians dead on the seashore*. This is the passage of scripture He breathed into my heart.

> "The waters returned and covered the chariots and the charioteers, and all the army of Pharaoh that had gone into the sea after them; not even one of them survived. But the Israelites walked on dry land in the middle of the sea, and the waters formed a wall to them on their right hand and on their left. The LORD saved Israel that day from the hand of the Egyptians, and Israel saw the Egyptians [lying] dead on the seashore."
>
> — Exodus 14:28-30, AMP

I had already crossed the Red Sea. I was His, but the Egyptians were still pursuing. God assured me that day—and He is assuring you now as well—you are safe in Him and dearly beloved. You are hidden in the cleft of the rock of the Lord Jesus, and eventually you will see all your enemies dead on the seashore. He has and will vanquish every foe.

> "And everyone who calls on the name of the Lord will be saved [saved, healed, and delivered]."
>
> — Acts 2:21 NIV, AMPLIFICATION ADDED

Who You Really Are

Although we may have picked up unhealthy tools to handle life's difficulties and developed habits that have marred the beauty of our true identity, it doesn't override or discredit or eliminate God's original design, our *imago*.

Who we really are is who He saw when He formed us in our mother's womb...and we are so treasured in His heart. Freedom comes as we experience more of His heart for us, hear His love words over us, and *begin to think as He thinks about us.*

Sometimes we develop such a negative inner self image that we are convinced that in order to be loved and lovable, we need to be made over almost into a different person. This is so seductive and deceiving because there is an element of truth to this mindset.

God *does* transform us, and we *do* become new creations when we are born again, but the lie is that God wants to change you into another person. No. He loves you so much. He is so committed to the restoration of His original design. He wants to reveal the beauty of who He created you to be. He has never changed His mind about you, and He never will.

You are changing your mind about you! You are learning to love yourself healthily by getting so close to His heart that you see yourself and others through His eyes of love. That revelation will change you, continually. And all the while you are safely covered, sheltered in His shadow of love and care, and hidden under His healing wings.

"But unto you that fear my name shall the Sun of righteousness arise with healing in his wings; and ye shall go forth, and grow up as calves of the stall."

— MALACHI 4:2, KJV

You are free from the accusation of the enemy, others, and even yourself. Though there may at times be glaring faults and failures, that's not the issue. He has covered you and removed your shame.

God is Love. We so often quote this that it has become cliché, but my prayer for you is that you will fully come to know Him as the unconditional lover of your soul. I pray that you will rediscover the secret place where He first encountered you and stamped you with His image...and that you will learn to abide there continually, not out of duty or fear, but out of passion and love.

I pray you will see what He saw when He imagined you, and that you will live out of that identity. That is His ultimate intention for you.

You interfaced with God when He formed you, and you will never be truly fulfilled or fulfill His plans until you allow Him to take you through the wondrous process of unveiling the beauty of who you really are. He alone has the keys that will unlock you and cause you to become the dream of His heart.

While you are in the process of being unveiled from glory to glory, you are securely *in Christ*, holy and complete.

That's who you really are.

Unveiled and loved.

Unveiled and safe.

Unveiled and beautiful.

Unveiled and glorious.

APPENDIX — BIBLE STUDY QUESTIONS

Chapter 1

Bible Study Questions:

- The adult stage of a butterfly is the Imago or image. The image is in the DNA of the creature from the beginning; it is just not revealed until its transformation. What are some lessons that you can take to heart from this natural example?

Check out these amazing nature facts: Most authorities agree that there are more insect species that have not been described (named by science) than there are insect species that have been previously named. Conservative estimates suggest that this figure is 2 million, but estimates extend to 30 million.[1] There are 228,450 known species in the ocean

— and as many as 2 million more that remain a total mystery.[2] There are approximately 20,000 species of butterflies in the world.[3] If God was so diverse and creative in the creation of mere fish and insects, how do you think He feels about the uniqueness of His children? How does He feel about your own unique personality, abilities, and characteristics? How does that make you feel?

- Read Psalm 139. Write down what this shows you about the Father's heart toward you.

- Since God knew you *before* He formed you, is it possible for the circumstances of your birth to have been accidental or coincidental?

- Read Jeremiah 1:4-10, Exodus 2:1-10, Exodus 3:1-12, and 1 Samuel 1:8-28. From these examples what can we assume about the timing of the call of God?

- Read John 15:16. Why do you think it was important to Jesus for you to know that He initiated the relationship He has with you?

- Read Isaiah 46:10, Revelations 1:8, and Revelations 22:13. What do these verses teach us about God's ability to accomplish His purposes and plans?

- Since Jesus initiated His relationship with you, and He always accomplishes His good pleasure (Isaiah 46:10), how secure should you feel in His faithfulness to His dream for your life?

- "Arise, shine; for your light has come, And the glory of the LORD has risen upon you. 'For behold, darkness will cover the earth And deep darkness the peoples; But the LORD will rise upon you And His glory will appear upon you'" (Isaiah 60:1-2 NASB). According to this passage, how will God fill the earth with His glory?

Notes

Chapter 2

Bible Study Questions:

- Take some time and really examine your daily walk, your choices. List some behaviors that constitute unhealthy or even sinful patterns in which you feel stuck.

- Read Genesis 4:7, Romans 6:17-18, Colossians 2:13, and Romans 8:13. In regards to real victory over sin, what is Jesus's part and your part in attaining freedom?

- Science even agrees with the truth of scripture. What the Bible calls renewing the mind, science calls neuroplasticity. This is basically the understanding that the human brain changes. Think of your brain as soft clay and your thoughts as the fingers that mold the clay. Your thoughts change your brain! Or, as we know from the Bible, "As [a man] thinks in his heart, so is he" (Prov. 23:7a, NKJV).

- Prayerfully choose a few scriptures that need to go from your head to your heart. Write them here, and intentionally, consistently meditate on them daily.

- Just as with Simon Peter, revelation knowledge is something that God builds upon. It is tied to overcoming all of hell's power and links us to the authority to do the kingdom work of binding and loosing on earth.

- Read Psalms 25:14; Isaiah 22:22-23; and Exodus 33:12-22. What connections do you see between intimacy with God and kingdom authority? What are some practical applications and outcomes of this in your own life?

- What happens in our soul when we feed it with the Word

of God? Read Psalms 19:7-14 in TPT. List the specific benefits to your soul.

- Read Matthew 7:21-27; Psalm 18:2 (TPT); and Exodus 33:21 (TLV). Who and what is the rock we stand upon? What are the benefits of the life that is built upon that rock? In these passages what are the markers of a life with a firm foundation?

- Read Psalm 33:1-6 and Psalm 51:6. If lies, deception, and hypocrisy are in our inward parts, what are the effects on our life? What happens when we repent and embrace truth? What does wisdom look like in a human life?

- Read 1 Peter 2:2; Proverbs 27:7; Psalm 119:165; and John 1:8. What can hunger for God and His word safeguard us from?

- Read Proverbs 11:2; Job 40:4 (MSG); and Psalm 131:2 (TPT). Take a moment and pray for God to open your heart and mind to truth that you currently "know not". Humble your heart. Lay down all pride, including spiritual pride, that tells us we already know it all. Ask God to make you like a child in your hunger, humility, and teachability. Expect for Him to show you great and mighty things in the days ahead!

- Read Colossians 3:10; Romans 12:2; Psalm 119:171; Ephesians 4:23; and Psalm 119:9-11. What is the catalyst and key to the renewal process?

- Read Psalm 91 and consider the precious words: dwell, secret place, shelter, shadow, and list any other "protection words" and phrases that you see. Read it in a few other translations, and see if your word list grows.

- If you make the secret place your abode, how safe are you during the process of transformation?

Notes

Chapter 3

Bible Study Questions:

- One tactic the enemy uses to keep us stuck is to make us feel that there are things in our lives that will never change. Life experiences, repeated failures, and fears reiterate this lie until it is a figurative mountain before us! Read Mark 11:23; Matthew 21:21; and Matthew 17:20 (TPT). Compare your issue (your mountain) to the size of your Jesus. Ask the Lord to increase your faith.

- Read Luke 17:5-8 and James 2:14-22 (TPT). How is faith proven, activated?

- Read Romans 10:17 (AMP and TPT). How is faith increased?

- Read Revelation 19:13; Psalms 119:89; Luke 16:17 (TPT); Exodus 12:1-30 (NIV); and John 5:53-58 (TPT). Who is the Word of God? How do we consume Him?

- Read Luke 8:14 (TPT). According to this verse, what things in general keep you from the maturity you long for? What specific thing(s) in your life has the Holy Spirit been showing you is spoiling your fruitfulness?

- Let's look at this verse together: "You must catch the troubling foxes, those sly little foxes that hinder our relationship. For they raid our budding vineyard of love to ruin what I've planted within you. Will you catch them and remove them for me? We will do it together" (Song of Songs 2:15, TPT). How passionate is the Lord Jesus about your vineyard (your fruitful relationship) with Him?

- He asks in this passage, "Will you catch them and remove them for me?" Can you hear Him asking you this heartfelt question? Give Him your answer. Take extra notice of His promise to you, the last line of the verse, "We will do it together." Hide that word in your heart today! Your love King, the living Word of God, the One who desires to make you His fruitful vine, promises to conquer your issues together!

Notes

Chapter 4

Bible Study Questions:

- We are in the army of God, and we do spiritual battle. Read Romans 8:37. Is defeat (or cycles of defeat) a part of our warfare? What does you being more than a conqueror say about the power of any enemy you face?

- Read Colossians 2:15. Does the enemy have any weapons? Does he have any authority? Does he have any power or legal right to accuse?

- Read 2 Corinthians 10:3-4. Describe your weapons.

- Read Luke 10:19. Describe your authority.

- Read Colossians 2:10-15. Describe your legal right to stand unashamed before God.

- Read Ephesians 4:27. Is it possible to give place (ground, access, or opportunity) to the devil? According to Ephesians chapter 4, what are some examples of ways we give him access? How important then is your obedience?

- Taken together, what can we say about our responsibility in living as an overcomer and more than a conqueror?

- You may now be thinking, "But no one is perfect! I thought Jesus won my victory!" YES! Read this: "But if we keep living in the pure light that surrounds him, we share unbroken fellowship with one another, and the blood of Jesus, his Son, continually cleanses us from all sin. If we boast that we have no sin, we're only fooling ourselves and are strangers to the truth. But if we freely admit our sins when his light uncovers them, he will be faithful to forgive us every time. God is just to forgive us our sins because of Christ, and he will continue to cleanse us from all unrighteousness. If we claim that we're not guilty of sin when God uncovers it with his light, we make him a liar and his word is not in us" (1 John 1:7-10). According to this passage, how do we remain continually cleansed? What if we do sin (verse nine)? According to verse ten, what is the way to respond when God's light (His Word and Spirit) exposes your sin?

- Lastly, consider that in Psalm 136 the phrase "His love endures forever" is repeated twenty-six times. Twenty-six is the numerical value of God's name, Yahweh. It is who He is. He is a faithful God! If hope is dwindling in your heart today, then check out what you are putting your hope in. Put your hope in His FAITHFULNESS! God cannot fail and will certainly never fail in His love for you, even if you fail miserably. He will never change his mind about you!

Notes

Chapter 5

Bible Study Questions:

- Read Job 1:1-6 and 1 Cor 10:13. Who is in charge (not the source) of our trials? Can Satan do as he pleases in the life of a believer? What are his limits?

- Ephesians 4:27 says, "Leave no [such] room or foothold for the devil [give no opportunity to him]" (Ephesians 4:27, AMPC). Paul wrote this exhortation to believers he was calling to walk with God in holiness and truth. The room or place he was referring to was the heart and life of the Christian. The warning rings clearly: don't give the enemy access to your life. Who gives the enemy legal ground in your life?

- Read Genesis 4:3-7. What is crouching at the door?

- Read Romans chapter 6. How do we rule over sin?

- As we discussed in this chapter, when we have a need, and we choose to have it met, we basically have three options. We can bring it to God and let him fill it, we can attempt to meet the need in our own strength, or we choose to accept Satan's counterfeit, or substitute, to fill our need. Read Hebrews 11:25 and Romans 6:23. Even though sin gives us a temporary relief, it only leads to death and slavery to more sin. Look at Psalm 23 verses 1-3: "The Lord is my best friend and my shepherd. I always have more than enough. He offers a resting place for me in his luxurious love. His tracks take me to an oasis of peace, the quiet brook of bliss. That's where he restores and revives my life. He opens before me pathways to God's pleasure and leads me along in his footsteps of righteousness so that I can bring honor to his name." What does this passage reveal about how God wants to meet our deepest needs?

- Can we recognize the greater plan of our adversary? Indeed. He is after something very precious: our intimacy with God. He knows sin brings death and separation, and so he is looking, crouching at the door even, for an opportunity to take a piece of our heart away from pure devotion to God. How do we safeguard our hearts from his schemes? We must stay aflame with fiery love for Jesus. Read Song of Songs 4:7-12, 15 and ask God to set His seal of fiery love upon your heart once more!

Notes

Chapter 6

Bible Study Questions:

- "Jesus said to them, 'Listen. No one is able to break into a mighty man's house and steal his property unless he first overpowers the mighty man and ties him up. Then his entire house can be plundered and his possessions taken'" (Mark 3:27, TPT). In order for the enemy to steal from you (joy, peace, loving connections, prosperity, health, etc.) what must he do first?

- "'I speak eternal truth,' Jesus said. 'When you sin you are not free. You've become a slave in bondage to your sin. And slaves have no permanent standing in a family, like a son does, for a son is a part of the family forever. So if the Son sets you free from sin, then become a true son and be unquestionably free!'" (John 8:34-36, TPT). "For if you embrace the truth, it will release true freedom into your lives" (John 8:32, TPT). "Your Word is truth! So make them holy by the truth" (John 17:17, TPT). According to these verses, how is slavery and bondage broken?

- If truth frees us (John 8:32), what binds us? Refer also to this passage: "...He's [the devil's] been a murderer right from the start! He never stood with the truth, for he's full of nothing but lies—lying is his native tongue. He is a master of deception and the father of lies! But I am the true Prince who speaks nothing but the truth" (John 8:44-45, TPT).

- What are some lies that may come into our hearts when we experience traumas such as abuses, near-death experiences, illness, accidents, mistreatment by leaders/authority figures, neglect, abandonment, or humiliation? (For example: God doesn't care about my pain.)

- When we dismantle these lies and replace them with God's truth, we remove the enemy's access to our house.[4] How important then is it for us to read and apply God's word?

- "Now you understand that I have imparted to you all my authority to trample over his kingdom. You will trample upon every demon before you and overcome every power Satan possesses. Absolutely nothing will be able to harm you as you walk in this authority. However, your real source of joy isn't merely that these spirits submit to your authority, but that your names are written in the journals of heaven and that you belong to God's kingdom. This is the true source of your authority" (Luke 10:19-20, TPT). How much of His authority has Jesus imparted to you? What is the source of this authority? As you walk in this authority, how powerful is the enemy over you to harm you?

Notes

Chapter 7

Bible Study Questions:

- Read Matthew chapter 18. List each person and thing in the parable as well as what they represent (i.e. the king represents Jesus, the debt represents sin, the prison represents unforgiveness, etc.).

- After studying Jesus teaching on the kingdom mindset of forgiveness in Matthew 18, do you see anyone who is exempt from the need to forgive and be forgiven?

- In that parable, who put the servant in prison? Who was the one responsible (through his choices) for the imprisonment? How could he have remained free?

- "Never hold a grudge or try to get even, but plan your life around the noblest way to benefit others. Do your best to live as everybody's friend. Beloved, don't be obsessed with taking revenge, but leave that to God's righteous justice. For the Scriptures say: 'Vengeance is mine, and I will repay,' says the Lord. And: If your enemy is hungry, buy him lunch! Win him over with kindness. For your surprising generosity will awaken his conscience, and God will reward you with favor. Never let evil defeat you, but defeat evil with good" (Romans 12:17-21 TPT). What are the key points in this verse?

- Look at these verses: "Speak blessing, not cursing, over those who reject and persecute you" (Romans 12:14 TPT). "Your words are so powerful that they will kill or give life..." (Proverbs 18:21, TPT). Taken together, what does this teach us about the power we have as believers to bring the kingdom, will, and redemptive plan of God into bad situations and into the lives of even those who hurt us?

- Lastly, read about the life of Joseph in Genesis 37-50 and his amazing story of betrayal, forgiveness, and redemption. Meditate especially on this passage: "And Joseph said to them, Fear not; for am I in the place of God? [Vengeance is His, not mine.] As for you, you thought evil against me, but God meant it for good, to bring about that many people should be kept alive, as they are this day. Now therefore, do not be afraid. I will provide for and support you and your little ones. And he comforted them [imparting cheer, hope, strength] and spoke to their hearts [kindly]" (Genesis 50:19-21, AMPC). Write down the truths God reveals to you in this story about the power of mercy and forgiveness.

Notes

Chapter 8

Bible Study Questions:

- Read James 4:10-12 and Romans 14:4. According to these verses who is the only Judge of human hearts?

- Romans 14:4 declares one of the reasons that we are not allowed to judge fellow servants is because we are not the master. It is understood that the master will take care of and help his own servant. Does it bless you to know that God feels this way about His servants? Why?

- Let's take a look at the story of the woman caught in adultery: "Then in the middle of his teaching, the religious scholars and the Pharisees broke through the crowd and brought a woman who had been caught in the act of committing adultery and made her stand in the middle of everyone. Then they said to Jesus, 'Teacher, we caught this woman in the very act of adultery. Doesn't Moses' law command us to stone to death a woman like this? Tell us, what do you say we should do with her?' They were only testing Jesus because they hoped to trap him with his own words and accuse him of breaking the laws of Moses. But Jesus didn't answer them. Instead he simply bent down and wrote in the dust with his finger. Angry, they kept insisting that he answer their question, so Jesus stood up and looked at them and said, 'Let's have the man who has never had a sinful desire throw the first stone at her.' And then he bent over again and wrote some more words in the dust. Upon hearing that, her accusers slowly left the crowd one at a time, beginning with the oldest to the youngest, with a convicted conscience. Until finally, Jesus was left alone with the woman still standing there in front of him. So he stood back up and said to her, 'Dear woman, where are your accusers? Is there no one here to condemn you?' Looking around, she replied, 'I see no one, Lord.' Jesus said, 'Then I certainly don't condemn you either. Go, and from now on, be free from a life of sin.' Then Jesus said, I am light to the world and those who embrace me will experience life-giving light, and they will never walk in darkness" (John 8:3-12, TPT).

Who is the only one qualified to condemn?

- Study this familiar passage from John 3: "For this is how much God loved the world—he gave his one and only, unique Son as a gift. So now everyone who believes in him will never perish but experience everlasting life. God did not send his Son into the world to judge and condemn the world, but to be its Savior and rescue it! So now there is no longer any condemnation for those who believe in him, but the unbeliever already lives under condemnation because they do not believe in the name of God's beloved Son. And here is the basis for their judgment: The Light of God has now come into the world, but the hearts of people love their darkness more than the Light, because they want the darkness to conceal their evil" (John 3:16-19, TPT). Who does not live under condemnation and judgment? Who does? What is the basis for their judgment?

- According to John 3:19, people come under judgment when they love darkness, evil, and evil deeds. Read Matthew 12:33-37 and Proverbs 21:4. According to these verses, what should we judge (rather than a person's heart)?

- This is another extremely helpful passage: "If you do not sit in judgment of others, you will avoid judgment yourself. But when we are judged, it is the Lord's training so that we will not be condemned along with the world" (1 Corinthians 11:31-32, TPT). What keeps you from coming under judgment? When we are judged, what is God's motive?

Notes

Chapter 9

Bible Study Questions:

- "An undeserved curse will be powerless to harm you. It may flutter over you like a bird, but it will find no place to land" (Proverbs 26:2 TPT). According to this verse, a curse must have a cause—it must be deserved. Look again at this list of causes:

1. All forbidden, aberrant, or unlawful sexual relationships
2. Anti-Semitism
3. Dependence on human strength, wisdom or goodness
4. Words spoken by those in authority
5. Stealing and lying
6. Words spoken against ourselves
7. Oaths or covenants taken for admission into secret societies and ungodly organizations
8. Curses pronounced by witches, occultists or witchdoctors
9. Carnal talk directed at others
10. Witchcraft prayer (manipulative)
11. Disrespect and disobedience to parents
12. Acknowledging or worshipping false gods
13. Involvement with the occult
14. Mistreating the weak and defenseless

- Go through this list prayerfully and repent of any participation you have had in them. Ask the Lord to remove the resulting curses from your life and bloodline. It might look like this prayer:

I confess the sins of my ancestors and my own sins of _____. I ask for Your forgiveness from these sins. I forgive myself and my ancestors for these sins and for the resulting curses. I ask you Lord to deliver me and my descendants from these sins

and from their consequences in my life and in the lives of my
descendants to a thousand generations. As you remove these curses from
my life, what blessing(s) would you like to give me in exchange?
Receive His blessing.

- Do a study on each of those causes and find the scriptural
  reference for each one.

- Here are some amazing Bible promises concerning your
  future generations. Study them, pray them, and believe
  them for yourself and your family to a thousand
  generations!

"All your children shall be taught by the LORD, and great
shall be the peace of your children" (Isaiah 54:13 ESV).

"'And as for me, this is my covenant with them,' says the
LORD: 'My Spirit that is upon you, and my words that I
have put in your mouth, shall not depart out of your mouth,
or out of the mouth of your offspring, or out of the mouth
of your children's offspring,' says the LORD, 'from this time
forth and forevermore'" (Isaiah 59:21 ESV).

"For I will pour water on the thirsty land, and streams on the
dry ground; I will pour my Spirit upon your offspring, and
my blessing on your descendants. They shall spring up
among the grass like willows by flowing streams. This one
will say, 'I am the LORD's,' another will call on the name of
Jacob, and another will write on his hand, 'The LORD's,'
and name himself by the name of Israel" (Isaiah 44:3-5
ESV).

"...I will make an everlasting covenant with them. Their
offspring shall be known among the nations, and their
descendants in the midst of the peoples; all who see them
shall acknowledge them, that they are an offspring the
LORD has blessed" (Isaiah 61:8-9 ESV).

"They shall not labor in vain or bear children for calamity, for they shall be the offspring of the blessed of the LORD, and their descendants with them" (Isaiah 65:23 ESV).

"I will give them one heart and one way, that they may fear me forever, for their own good and the good of their children after them" (Jeremiah 32:39 ESV).

"Therefore you shall keep his statutes and his commandments, which I command you today, that it may go well with you and with your children after you, and that you may prolong your days in the land that the LORD your God is giving you for all time" (Deuteronomy 4:40 ESV).

- Here is a sample prayer:

Lord Jesus, you have promised your people that all our children shall be taught by the Lord. Please do this! Please reveal yourself to all my children and grandchildren and descendants and bring each one into peace with you through your blood.

- Look up each one of these verses for further study:

Acts 16:31-33
Proverbs 20:7
Proverbs 14:26
Psalms 102:28
Psalms 112:1-2

Notes

Chapter 10

Bible Study Questions:

- Read through the entire book of Job, in light of our discussion in this chapter.

- With his story as an example, identify and describe how each of these things relate to you and your trial.

  1. God's sovereignty

  2. God's faithful hand in charge of the trial

  3. Job's greatest fear

  4. Job's need for transformation

  5. The voice(s) of men

  6. The voice of the enemy

  7. God's voice

  8. Job's discoveries in the fire of his trial

- What insights can you take from Job's story and apply to your own life, circumstances, relationships, difficulties, etc.? Be specific.

- What pitfalls of his can you avoid?

- What encouragement can you take to heart?

Notes

Chapter 11

Bible Study Questions:

- If we are living in full assurance of the love of our shepherd, then we see several amazing results. Take a walk through Psalm 23, and see these benefits of abiding in His fold:

1. I shall not want. I am satisfied. I shall not lust.
2. When I need comfort and peace (green pastures, still waters), He will supply.
3. When my soul is malfunctioning, he restores it.
4. When I go through life's stinkiest of times, He is with me to guide and comfort me. I am NEVER ALONE.
5. When others may have excluded or mistreated me, He will throw me a big ol' party right in front of them, and they will be forced to watch me get His blessing. When there is warfare all around me, I can feast on the goodness of His presence and be sustained.
6. His plan for me is to live in the abundance of His anointing...so much so, that it overflows to all that surrounds me.
7. When I blow it, I don't have to run and hide, because His mercy and unconditional love are always chasing me down to make me right and whole again.
8. Finally, in the end, I win, because I am a daughter or son of God living with Him forever!

- Look at these verses about the brooks of bliss that we are meant to drink from continually:

"For you bring me a continual revelation of resurrection life, the path to the bliss that brings me face-to-face with you" (Psalms 16:11, TPT).

"He offers a resting place for me in his luxurious love. His tracks take me to an oasis of peace, the quiet brook of bliss" (Psalms 23:2, TPT).

"When there is no clear prophetic vision, people quickly wander astray. But when you follow the revelation of the word, heaven's bliss fills your soul" (Proverbs 29:18, TPT).

"What bliss you experience when your heart is pure! For then your eyes will open to see more and more of God" (Matthew 5:8, TPT).

"And they will depart from his presence and go into eternal punishment. But the godly and beloved 'sheep' will enter into eternal bliss" (Matthew 25:46, TPT).

"He will be standing firm like a flourishing tree planted by God's design, deeply rooted by the brooks of bliss, bearing fruit in every season of his life. He is never dry, never fainting, ever blessed, ever prosperous" (Psalms 1:3, TPT).

"I long to bring you to my innermost chamber— this holy sanctuary you have formed within me. O that I might carry you within me. I would give you the spiced wine of my love, this full cup of bliss that we share. We would drink our fill . . . "(Song of Songs 8:2, TPT).

"Wonderfully blessed are those who wash their robes white so they can access the Tree of Life and enter the city of bliss by its open gates" (Revelation 22:14, TPT).

- After reading these verses, thoughtfully and prayerfully answer these questions:

  - How would you describe the bliss God intends for His people?

- Why does He want you to experience this bliss?

- What is the opposite of bliss?

- Have you settled for less than bliss?

- Why do you think the enemy wants to keep you from bliss (empty, lacking, lusting, sad, lonely, thirsty, etc.)?

- What are the practical ways for you to continually drink from the brooks of bliss?

Notes

Chapter 12

Bible Study Questions:

Read these selections of verses, and for each one, write the revelation you receive about Father.

Protection:

Exodus 14:21-31

Psalm 91

Psalm 121:1-3

Thessalonians 3:3

Isaiah 54:17

Isaiah 26:3-4

Isaiah 43:1-7

John 17:11

Provision:

John 3:16

James 1:17

Romans 24

Romans 8:32

Luke 12:31

2 Corinthians 9:10

Acts 17:24-26

Philippians 4:19

Identity:

Romans 9:25

Psalm 60:6

Luke 15:31

Mark 1:11

2 Corinthians 6:18

Luke 15:22

Notes

Chapter 13

Bible Study Questions:

Jesus is a beautiful friend. Look at these aspects of His nature that make Him the *best friend* we could ever have, and write down your thoughts on each one.

- Jesus loves you to the highest degree: *"For the greatest love of all is a love that sacrifices all. And this great love is demonstrated when a person sacrifices his life for his friends"* (John 15:13, TPT).

- Jesus will never be unfaithful to you: *"Then I saw heaven opened, and suddenly a white horse appeared. The name of the one riding it was Faithful and True, and with pure righteousness he judges and rides to battle"* (Revelation 19:11 TPT).

- Jesus wants to share deep intimacy with you: *"I have never called you 'servants,' because a master doesn't confide in his servants, and servants don't always understand what the master is doing. But I call you my most intimate friends, for I reveal to you everything that I've heard from my Father"* (John 15:15, TPT).

- Jesus wants you to become like Him: *"A pupil is not superior to his teacher, but everyone [when he is] completely trained (readjusted, restored, set to rights, and perfected) will be like his teacher"* (Luke 6:40, AMPC).

- Jesus wants you to be just as close to His Dad as He is! *"For the very glory you have given to me I have given them so that they will be joined together as one and experience the same unity that we enjoy. You live fully in me and now I live fully in them so that they will experience perfect unity, and the world will be convinced that you have sent me, for they will see that you love each one of them with the same passionate love that you have for me. Father, I ask that you allow everyone that you have given to me to be with me where I am! Then they will see my full glory— the very splendor you have placed upon me because you have loved me even before the beginning of time. You are my righteous Father, but the unbelieving world has never known you in the perfect way that I know you! And all those who believe in me also know that you have sent me! I have revealed to them who you are and I will continue to make you even more real to them, so that they may experience the same endless love that you have for me, for your love will now live in them, even as I live in them!"* (John 17:22-26, TPT).

- Jesus really wants to be with you. You don't have to beg or wistfully long for His time and attention. In fact, it is quite the opposite: *"After this I let my devotion slumber, but my heart for him stayed awake. I had a dream. I dreamed of my beloved— he was coming to me in the darkness of night. The melody of the man I love awakened me. I heard his knock at my heart's door as he pleaded with me: Arise, my love. Open your heart, my darling, deeper still to me. Will you receive me this dark night? There is no one else but you, my friend, my equal. I need you this night to arise and come be with me. You are my pure, loyal dove, a perfect partner for me. My flawless one, will you arise? For my heaviness and tears are more than I can bear. I have spent myself for you throughout the dark night"* (Song of Songs 5:2, TPT).

- You are His favorite: *"I could have chosen any from among the vast multitude of royal ones who follow me. But one is my beloved dove—unrivaled in beauty, without equal, beyond compare, the perfect one, the favorite one. Others see your beauty and sing of your joy. Brides and queens chant your praise: 'How blessed is she!'"* (Song of Songs 6:8-9, TPT).

- He is perfect in every way! No one can compare to Him: *"Most sweet are his kisses, even his whispers of love. He is delightful in every way and perfect from every viewpoint. If you ask me why I love him so, O brides-to-be, it's because there is none like him to me. Everything about him fills me with holy desire! And now he is my beloved—my friend forever"* (Song of Songs 5:16 TPT).

- Jesus is full of life and adventure! He wants you to step out of the constricting boats of life and walk on water (do the impossible) with Him! He has all the answers, but He doesn't reveal it all at once. Instead, He wants to lead you on adventures of discovery! This is who He is: *"Then Jesus turned around and saw they were following him and asked, 'What do you want?' They responded, 'Rabbi (which means, Master Teacher), where are you staying?' Jesus answered, 'Come and discover for yourselves.' So they went with him and saw where he was staying, and since it was late in the afternoon, they spent the rest of the day with Jesus"* (John 1:38-39, TPT).

- In Psalm 136, the phrase "His love endures forever" is repeated twenty-six times. Twenty-six is the numerical value of God's name, Yahweh. It is WHO HE IS. A faithful God! If hope is dwindling in your heart today, then check out where you are putting it. Hope in His FAITHFULNESS! He cannot fail and will certainly never fail in His love for you even if you fail miserably. He will never change His mind about you! How does this inspire you?

Notes

Chapter 14

Bible Study Questions:

- Read John 3:3-13. How is the Holy Spirit and also those born of Him described?

- Nicodemus wanted to catch the wind with his natural mind, but Jesus brought the understanding that the Spirit is not caught intellectually. Have you been caught up in the Spirit? If so, describe how your faith wings had to be extended in order for you to catch the Spirit-wind.

- "And without faith living within us it would be impossible to please God. For we come to God in faith knowing that he is real and that he rewards the faith of those who passionately seek him" (Hebrews 11:6, TPT).

- When Holy Spirit comes, everything changes! All the power of heaven comes in Him. Do a little study of the gifts of the Spirit in 1 Corinthians 12-14. List the gifts, and describe them.

- Holy Spirit also produces His fruit in and through our lives. By this fruit, the world around us (family, friends, community) experiences His amazing goodness. Read Galatians 5, and identify or list the fruit of the Spirit. Ask for each one to be more developed in your life!

- God's Spirit is sometimes revealed in scripture as His wrap-around presence. He is our security blanket that surrounds us at all times. Look at these verses and then describe what it means to you personally that God is surrounding you.

"Because you are close to me and always available, my confidence will

never be shaken, for I experience your wrap-around presence every moment" (Psalms 16:8 TPT).

"The lovers of God will be glad, rejoicing in the Lord. They will be found in his glorious wrap-around presence, singing songs of praise to God!" (Psalms 64:10 TPT).

"God's glory is all around me! His wrap-around presence is all I need, for the Lord is my Savior, my hero, and my life-giving strength" (Psalms 62:7 TPT).

"You empower me for victory with your wrap-around presence. Your power within makes me strong to subdue, and by stooping down in gentleness you strengthened me and made me great!" (Psalms 18:35 TPT).

- Jesus promised His disciples (and with them, all believers) this: "And I will send you the Divine Encourager from the very presence of my Father. He will come to you, the Spirit of Truth, emanating from the Father, and he will speak to you about me" (John 15:26, TPT). List the attributes and work of Holy Spirit revealed in this one verse. What does this mean to you?

- Just before leaving this world, Jesus said to his disciples, "...And never forget that I am with you every day, even to the completion of this age" (Matthew 28:20, TPT). Jesus is forever God and Man. He cannot *physically* be with all believers all the time. How has this precious promise been fulfilled through the person of the Holy Spirit? What does it speak to your heart that Jesus made this important declaration before leaving?

Notes

Chapter 15

Bible Study Questions:

- Read John 7:37-38 and John 8:32. According to these verses what is the source of freedom? Instead of striving or working harder at changing ourselves, what are we encouraged to do?

- Read 1 Corinthians 1:26-31. From where do we draw our life? In union with Jesus, transformation of our souls takes place, therefore what is our boast?

- Read John 15:4, Hebrews 13:21, and Romans 8:1. From these verses, describe the results of life union, intimate fellowship with Christ.

- According to Ephesians 6:10, where does the strength and power for true freedom flow from?

- The purpose of this lesson is to perhaps expose lies we may be believing that are hindering the union with Jesus for which we long and for which we are created. From your own times of intimate connection with the Lord, describe what happens in His presence.

- This love connection, simply abiding in Him, is meant to be continuous. Read John 15:1-5. Ask the Lord to reveal to you any lie you may be believing that is hindering your abiding and keeping you from His life-flow that produces the fruit, life, and power you are designed to have.

- Prayer: *Lord, is there any lie I am believing about You? What truth do You want me to know about You? What lie is hurting my intimacy with You? What truth do You want me to know about myself?*

- Write down what He speaks and meditate on the truths revealed. This is medicine for your wounds.

Notes

Chapter 16

Bible Study Questions:

- Read 1 Corinthians 15:25, Luke 20:42-43, and Hebrews 10:12:14. What is Christ's current position? What is happening to His enemies? How long will He remain seated? Who then is trampling His enemies and placing them under His feet?

- In those passages, what does "until" refer to? What should you do (believe, pray, and behave) *until* your enemies are subdued?

- Read James 4:7. What do we do if the enemy is not yet subdued? Is there any place for passivity?

- In the case of James 4:7, what would be the result of passivity? Would the resulting defeat be God's fault? What does this speak to your heart about putting your foes under foot?

- Read Luke 10:19. Who tramples and by whose authority do they trample?

- Taking all of these passages together, when you trample the enemy under your feet, are you also putting him under Christ's feet? How does this revelation give explanation (in part) to Jesus's great rejoicing in Luke 10:21?

- Read Isaiah 53. List every individual benefit you have been given through Christ's suffering atonement.

Notes

Chapter 17

Bible Study Questions:

- The Hebrew Word for kiss is *nashaq*. This same word can be translated as kindle and armor. What does this reveal to you about the power and importance of intimate, face to face communion with the Lord?

- Jesus said this in Luke 10:19: "Now you understand that I have imparted to you all my authority to trample over his kingdom. You will trample upon every demon before you and overcome every power Satan possesses. Absolutely nothing will be able to harm you as you walk in this authority" (Luke 10:19 TPT). How is our intimacy with God connected to our protection from harm? (See also Psalm 91.)

- Read Psalm 5:3. How are you a sacrificial offering to God? What does laying out your life piece by piece on the altar mean to you, personally?

- After reading about the sacrifice of Elijah in 1 Kings 18 and Abraham worshipping on Moriah in Genesis 22, describe what type of sacrifice brings down God's fire?

- Read Matthew 3:11-12 and Acts 2. "He will submerge you into union with the Spirit of Holiness and with a raging fire!" Have you experienced that baptism of fire in your own life? Describe your experience and what is has meant to you. If you haven't received the baptism of fire, simply ask and receive! It is for you today.

- Has your fire dimmed? After studying this lesson, what

have you learned you can you do to rekindle your fiery
passion for the Lord?

Notes

Chapter 18

Bible Study Questions:

- Read Revelations 22:1; Ezekiel 47:1; Isaiah 44:3; And Isaiah 58:11. Describe this River of Life. What is its source?

- John 7:38 says, "Believe in me so that rivers of living water will burst out from within you, *flowing* from your innermost being, just like the Scripture says!" The phrase *from your innermost being* can be translated "from His throne" (TPT footnotes notes). Because of this, do you believe we can see our heart as His throne, the seat of His authority and dominion? If so, what does that truth reveal to you?

- According to John 7:38, we are meant for a flowing river, a flooding of His Spirit in and through our lives. What things hinder that flow? In your own life, what has been hindering the flow? As God reveals them to you, repent and break free.

- "When your soul is full, you turn down even the sweetest honey. But when your soul is starving, every bitter thing becomes sweet" (Proverbs 27:7. TPT). According to this verse, how does spiritual hunger relate to spiritual fullness? Do you think it is possible to "crowd out" the Holy Spirit in our lives? How can you personally make more room for Him, for His flow?

- We studied the word baptism in this lesson. It is the Greek Word *baptizo* (immersed, overwhelmed), not to be confused with *bapto* (dipped). Dipping is nice, but immersion (pickling) brings transformation. "And don't get drunk with wine, which is rebellion; instead be filled with the fullness of the Holy Spirit. And your hearts will overflow with a joyful song to the Lord Jehovah. Keep speaking to each other with words of Scripture, singing the Psalms with praises and spontaneous songs given by the Spirit!" (Ephesians 5:18-19, TPT). How does worship, singing scriptures, and singing in the spirit contribute to your "pickling" process for transformation?

- Read Song of Songs 5:1. How does your fullness become a blessing for others?

Notes

Chapter 19

Bible Study Questions:

- Read Psalm 139:15. This secret place is referring to the womb of your mother where you were formed. How does this idea of a womb also relate to the secret place of intimate connection with God? How does He form and reform you there?

- Read Matthew 6:17. Where does Father dwell? Why do you think He calls you to secret (hidden, private) devotion?

- According to Psalm 81:7, what is available in the secret place?

- Read Psalm 32:7, Psalm 31:20, and Psalm 91:9. Make a list of all the benefits of the safety of the secret place and what they mean to you personally.

- Read Psalm 27. Let's focus on a few key verses:

"In his shelter in the day of trouble, that's where you'll find me, for he hides me there in his holiness. He has smuggled me into his secret place, where I'm kept safe and secure—out of reach from all my enemies. Triumphant now, I'll bring him my offerings of praise, singing and shouting with ecstatic joy! Yes, listen and you can hear the fanfare of my shouts of praise to the Lord" (vv. 5-6).

"Lord, when you said to me, 'Seek my face,' my inner being responded, 'I'm seeking your face with all my heart'" (v. 8).

"My father and mother abandoned me. I'm like an orphan! But you took me in and made me yours" (v. 10).

"Here's what I've learned through it all: Don't give up; don't be impatient; be entwined as one with the Lord. Be brave and courageous" (v. 14).

- Can you picture your Heavenly Father, tucking you into His heart and smuggling you in the secret place? You were lost and alone, but He took you up. Your longing cries to be entwined and deeply connected to His heart please and bless Him. And He will never disappoint that longing! Spend some time reiterating this prayer to the Lord making it your own. Thank Him that He will surely answer your prayer for more of Him.

Notes

NOTES

2. He Restores My Soul

1. This is a conservative estimate. There are varying percentages given by experts, up to 95%.
2. See Lk. 12:32.
3. See Rom. 14:17.
4. See John 10:10.
5. See Jeremiah 33:3.

3. Ending Harmful Cycles

1. See 1 Corinthians 13.

Part II

1. See Song of Songs 1.

5. Access Point 1: Disobedience

1. See Romans 6:23.
2. See 2 Corinthians 5:21.

7. Access Point 3: Unforgiveness

1. See Matthew 18:22.
2. Malone, Henry. *Shadow Boxing: the Dynamic 2-5-14 Strategy to Defeat the Darkness within /CHenry Malone.* Vision Life Publications, 2004.
3. See Romans 8:28.

9. Access Point 5: Curses

1. Malone, Henry. *Shadow Boxing: the Dynamic 2-5-14 Strategy to Defeat the Darkness within /CHenry Malone.* Vision Life Publications, 2004.
2. Ballard, Larry. "MULTIGENERATIONAL LEGACIES – THE STORY OF JONATHAN EDWARDS." YWAM Family Ministries, December 4, 2018. https://www.ywam-fmi.org/news/multigenerational-legacies-the-story-of-jonathan-edwards/.

10. A Job Trial

1. "Eliphaz." SheKnows, August 22, 2018. https://www.sheknows.com/baby-names/name/eliphaz/.
2. "Bildad." SheKnows, August 22, 2018. https://www.sheknows.com/baby-names/name/bildad/.
3. "Zophar." SheKnows, August 22, 2018. https://www.sheknows.com/baby-names/name/zophar/.

   Wikipedia contributors, "Zophar," *Wikipedia, The Free Encyclopedia*, https://en.wikipedia.org/w/index.php?title=Zophar&oldid=958127999 (accessed June 28, 2021).
4. See Ephesians 6.
5. "Elihu." SheKnows, August 22, 2018. https://www.sheknows.com/baby-names/name/elihu/.
6. See Genesis 3:1.
7. See Luke 4:3.
8. See John 19:30 TPT. See TPT footnote.

11. Jesus Cares

1. See Romans 5:12.

Part III

1. See John 8:32.

12. A Healthy View of Father

1. Faith Church, Facebook post, May 15, 2020,
   https://www.facebook.com/permalink.php?id=127987917229364&story_fbid=3538476302847158

13. A Healthy View of Jesus

1. Credit to the Father Ladder teaching and tool from Bethel Sozo, Dawna Desilva and Teresa Leibscher.
2. Strong's Greek: 5479. χαρά (chara) -- joy, delight. Accessed June 28, 2021. https://biblehub.com/greek/5479.htm.
3. See Luke 9:22; Acts 7:26; and Mark 14:62 (noting just a few).

14. A Healthy View of Holy Spirit

1. "COMFORT: Definition of COMFORT by Oxford Dictionary on Lexico.com Also Meaning of COMFORT." Lexico Dictionaries | English. Lexico Dictionaries. Accessed June 28, 2021. https://www.lexico.com/en/definition/comfort.
2. "COMMUNION: Definition of COMMUNION by Oxford Dictionary on Lexico.com Also Meaning of COMMUNION." Lexico Dictionaries | English. Lexico Dictionaries. Accessed June 28, 2021. https://www.lexico.com/en/definition/communion.
3. "CONSOLATION: Definition of CONSOLATION by Oxford Dictionary on Lexico.com Also Meaning of CONSOLATION." Lexico Dictionaries | English. Lexico Dictionaries. Accessed June 28, 2021. https://www.lexico.com/en/definition/consolation.
4. Dawna Desilva and Teresa Liebscher, "Father Ladder," Bethel Sozo.

15. Three Things You Cannot Repent Of

1. See Romans 12.

Part IV

1. "For it is Christ's love that fuels our passion and motivates us, because we are absolutely convinced that he has given his life for all of us. This means all died with him, so that those who live should no longer live self-absorbed lives but lives that are poured out for him—the one who died for us and now lives again" (1 Corinthians 5:14-15, TPT).

16. A Powerful Promise

1. See Ephesians 6.
2. See Psalm 3.
3. Nicole Spector, "Smiling Tricks Your Brain into Happiness" (NBC News, Jan 9, 2018), https://www.nbcnews.com/better/health/smiling-can-trick-your-brain-happiness-boost-your-health-ncna822591.

18. His Flowing River

1. TPT footnotes.
2. Strong's Concordance, Greek, 907
3. from Strong's Concordance, Greek, 911
4. James Montgomery Boice, Bible Study Magazine, May 1989.
5. "Physics Tutorial: What Is a Wave?" The Physics Classroom. Accessed June 28, 2021. https://www.physicsclassroom.com/class/waves/Lesson-1/What-is-a-Wave.

19. Face to Face In The Secret Place

1. See Numbers 6:25.
2. See John 15.
3. Coram Deo. Accessed 11/17/2020. https://en.wikipedia.org/wiki/Coram_Deo

20. Your Unveiling Is At Hand

1. See TPT footnotes Genesis 1 and 2.

21. Freedom to Focus

1. See Matt 13:44; Ps 91:1; and 1 Pet 2:9.

Appendix — Bible Study Questions

1. Smithsonian Institute, https://www.si.edu/.
2. Alister Doyle, Reuters. Mar. 17, 2015, 2:38 PM.
3. N. American Butterfly Association, https://www.naba.org/.
4. See Mark 3:27.

ACKNOWLEDGMENTS

A special thank you to Jesus—because of You, this book was possible.

Thank you to my husband, Jeremiah—because of your loving support, this book was written.

ABOUT THE AUTHOR

Teresa Yancy and her husband Jeremiah make their home in beautiful East Texas with their four amazing children, two dogs, and one cat. Teaching is her "native language," and she has been speaking it for over thirty years through various avenues, teaching in both public and private school venues, children's ministry, summer school programs, as well as many years of successful homeschooling.

Passion for helping others also led Teresa through a season of training and education in the area of inner healing and deliverance ministry, including an in-depth internship program in that field. Experiencing a greater level of personal freedom and intimacy with God herself inspired a passion to help others find that same freedom, and she has given herself to ministering, writing, and speaking on that topic. Her book, *Unveiled by God, Discovering the Beauty of Who You Really Are,* is an overflow of that pursuit. She uses a loving yet power-packed approach with the goal of giving practical keys to help unlock others from their prisons of shame and fear into a more peaceful and intimate walk with God.

Teresa and Jeremiah also own a media/marketing agency called Grow My Social, a book writing course and membership called Unlocking Your Book, and a publishing company called Messenger Books. They also work with Passion & Fire Ministries, the ministry of Brian and Candice Simmons, lead translators of The Passion Translation. Connect with Teresa on Facebook at Facebook.com/jeremiahandteresayancy and find more of her inspiring content at teresayancy.com.

www.ingramcontent.com/pod-product-compliance
Lightning Source LLC
Chambersburg PA
CBHW070554100426
42744CB00006B/277